My gratitude and unconditional love to Steve, Mike, Bruce and Gen, and special thanks to Steve and Gen for their assistance, and to all the friends and critics who taught me that we're fortunate to live in a state and nation where we <u>can</u> have an opinion about everything ... and <u>should</u>. Also, special thanks to Dale Bohren, who published my thoughts on the trivial and serious human issues, and to Peg Curry, my inspiration and my friend, then and now.

Text © 2017 by Audrey Mathews Cotherman
Cover photo © 2017 by Gen E. Cotherman

All rights reserved. No part of this book may be reproduced or transmitted in any form or by any means, electronic or mechanical, including photocopying, recording or by any information storage and retrieval system, without permission of the publisher.

ISBN 978-0-692-90935-5

Copy Editors: Audrey M. Cotherman, Steven R. Cotherman and Gen E. Cotherman
Design: Gen E. Cotherman

Table of Contents

Chapter 1
Bullies and Bitches 2
Cool, Rad, Bad 4
Graduation Retrospect 6
Relationships? Really? 8
Charity or Entitlement? 10
The Dog Ate My Homework 12
Get On With It 14
Holding A Grudge 16
Is It the Guns or the Values? 18
Keep History 20
In Defense of a Closed Mind 22
Noblesse Oblige, Civility, Charity 24
Arts and Humanities: Basic to Community 26
Good Losers and Sour Grapes 28
Talking With Your Hands 30
Needed or Needy? 33
Here's A Tip 35
You're Grabbing What? 37

Chapter 2
Blowing in the Wind 40
Budgets and Bulbs 42
Culture and Poverty 45
Ahhhh, Equality 48
Elder-Hostile or Save Our Students? 50
Running the Red 52
You Know You're In Wyoming When 55
Litter Did I Know 57
Losing Wyoming 59
Storm Musings 61
Move Over? 63
Save the Honors 65
Speak Up 67
Too Much Charity? 69
People In Our Circumstances 71
Whaaat? 73
Memories Are For Later 75

Chapter 3
Behind the Veil 78
Celebrating Age 80
Christmas Favorites 82
What's Going On? 84
What Happened to the Middle? 86
Putting On Airs 88

Remember and Resolve 90
Rock On 93
Scream Away 95
That's Rude, Dude 97
Greetings or Not 100
The Sound of Silence 103
Defending Liberal Education 105
Time After Time 107
Waiting 109

Chapter 4
Backward or Forward? 112
Un-resolving Changes 115
Comfort, Comfort 117
I Go to the Hills 119
Capstones and Milestones 121
Don't Fence Me In 124
Being Left Behind 126
Lighten Up 128
The Rest of the Story 131
Finish Something 133
My Favorite Things 135
Random Thoughts 137
Spilling the Bucket 139
Thanks, But No Cooking 141
Abstract or Practical 143
Under Penalty of Law 145
The Wyoming Way 147

Chapter 5
And the Winner Is 150
But What Can You Do? 152
Clichés and Other Indiscretions 154
Creating A World-Class Education System 156
Did You Hear What I Heard? 159
History or Histrionics 161
Just Follow the Proverbs 163
Poverty and Learning 165
Say What??? 167
Gadgets, Widgets and Wonders 170
Silence Is Not Always a Virtue 173
Hearts or Humours 175
Way Back To School 177
Public Broadcasting: Our Better Selves 179
Common Standards, Common Values 182
Getting This Straight 185

CHAPTER 1

Bullies and Bitches

Because I own a gun, I receive letters from Anthony Bouchard, executive for Wyoming Gun Owners. Even the legislature protested his bullying, which says a lot. Lest you think I'm either a "gun grabber" or intend to wear a gun on my hip to public meetings, I assure you that I'm old-school. I grew up in northern Minnesota where a) we hunted for food, and b) people who intimidated others with guns were considered city-slickers who shouldn't be hunting. That meant that north woods natives usually hunted out of season in order not to risk getting shot by the city-slickers.

But that's another issue to tackle another day, or not at all. What the Bouchard letter triggered was a memory of some bullying I've encountered and sometimes challenged. To be clear, if a male challenges a bully, he's a hero; if a female challenges a bully, she's a bitch. I understand that, but shall proceed anyway.

One of my first encounters was in a rural schoolyard with a stream running through the playground. Sonny pushed me in several days in a row, and when I complained to my father, whose best friend was Sonny's father, he told me to hit him with anything I had. Since I was only in first grade, I hit him with my lunchbox (which I still regret, because I put a dent in my collectible Little Orphan Annie lunchbox).

My father approved, though my mother worried about whether I would grow up feminine enough. Years later, when I was stopped on the Lincoln summit after almost running into the back end of a slow-moving truck and camping trailer that pulled out at 40 mph in front of my new Thunderbird, which was going 70, a burly young woman wearing leather boots and a camouflage jacket asked me to get out of my car so she could beat me up for giving the finger to her father, the driver of the slow-moving truck. I assured her it was my thumb, but refused to get out of the car since she was younger, stronger and had back-up.

One afternoon on Casper Mountain, I was walking on a public road with Minnesota friends who were visiting Wyoming for the first time, when a fellow with a gun on his hip and his hand on the gun ran through the brush shouting for us to get off his property. I knew the location of his property since he inherited the land next to me and put up "No Trespassing" signs ... I already thought he was a jerk. When I got up under his nose and asked him if he was going to shoot me or hit me first, my Minnesota friends headed down the path. They had their Wyoming story.

My father taught me to stand up to bullies, and I tried to pass that on to my three sons and daughter. Admittedly, one of my sons seemed to look for a bar brawl or neighborhood shoving match, and the strongest son was inclined to simply laugh, but the third one, the oldest, had a sense of the aesthetic from an early age. So when he was chased home from East Junior High School the third time, I told him he had to stand his ground.

His efforts produced a black eye of which he was proud. What had mortified him, however, was when his little brother ran into the field, grabbed the bully's collar and said "Leave my big brother alone." He wasn't threatened again ... if you don't view ridicule as threatening.

Sometimes bullies win, at least temporarily. In the 1990s, two powerful legislators in Wyoming tried to intimidate the University of Wyoming to prevent them from hiring me. They failed. I was hired, but UW ran out of money in six months, which may have been a coincidence. Fortunately, it led to one of the best jobs I ever had at the University of Wisconsin.

Bullying can be verbal, but in a world of such violence, we would settle if it were only verbal. It's hard to know what constitutes verbal bullying when our society guarantees we can say almost anything so long as we understand that we can't do just anything.

It's possible that those who can't tolerate certain ideas are verbal bullies because they're afraid of getting outside their intellectual comfort zones, especially if they believe that their place in Heaven is assured by how many non-believers they kill or convert.

According to the Oxford Dictionary, bullying is intimidating or persecuting weaker people. The problem is that it isn't easy to determine whether an idea intimidates someone and it's almost impossible to determine whether they consider themselves weak. Intimidation may be in the eye of the beholder rather than the intention of the speaker.

Personally, I stand up to attempts to intimidate me intellectually more easily than I stand up to physical threats. Sometimes it may be wise to run. There's got to be a difference between being a physical bully and an intellectual one. Maybe it's that difference that can turn bitches into bullies, and heroes into cowards.

Cool, Rad, Bad

Not so long ago, the rich served an important function as the keepers of the civilized culture. True, they may have had aristocratic presumptions, but they modeled the behavior that helped people move from one class to another in a society they claimed was classless.

The rich taught us that if we wanted to move up in the world we should develop good table manners. It was appropriate to keep one hand on your lap, over your napkin, and to hold your fork between the index and middle finger and your thumb. If we didn't keep our mouths closed while chewing and slurped our soup, there was no way we would end up the CEO or second in command, or in the corner office. All job candidates were taken to dinner to make sure they were of the quality needed/wanted by the company.

A secretarial job in the big office was unlikely if the bodice disclosed more than a hint of cleavage, and the skirt hem exposed more than the lower leg. Slacks and jeans weren't allowed.

If you doubt my contention, watch old movies. Everyone had a penthouse. The men dressed in top hats and tails, or in suits with high-waisted trousers that had a permanent crease.

They had dinner parties where they waited for the hostess to take the first bite, toasted each other and thanked the waiters. They never put their elbows and arms on the table, nor wiped/washed a child's face with their napkins. They also didn't continue to feed a child with a runny nose or have them wipe it on their sleeves. They never changed the baby's diapers on the restaurant table.

They drank a lot and smoked a lot, and that's why prohibition failed. They hardly ever asked if someone wanted a brew and they always squirted soda in their hard liquor. Sophisticated people smoked pipes or cigarettes, rather than chewing tobacco or inhaling snuff.

Just as the word for good manners changed from "sophisticated" to "cool" to "rad" to "bad," so did the customs ... and the movies.

How the dress has changed; even the 1960s generation wouldn't have purchased jeans with holes in them. It may have been for the wrong reason, but women in the 1950s left enough to the imagination to give men some incentives for chivalrous seduction.

Table manners have changed so radically that dining in a restaurant is rarely a romantic evening gazing into each other's eyes between dainty bites. Dining now often consists of time to catch up on phone messages or texting. There's little ambiance when someone's holding his fork like a shovel in a clasped fist.

Dining out seems to consist of dodging toddlers who are left to careen around the restaurant, empty sugar packets and smear jelly on the table and chairs. Dining at home with friends using china, stemware and silver is as obsolete as a camera with film. Preparations were elaborate; the meat had to be marinated and cut at the table in front of everyone, and dessert, preferably something no one had ever tasted before, was required. Several drinks were served before dinner and again after, in case the new recipes were a disaster.

Not to be indelicate, but there was an unwritten rule, passed from the downstairs rather than the upstairs, that a kiss was expected on the third date, but not before. An engagement ring was expected prior to more intimacies, and not on the first date. Engagements rarely happened on the first date, except in war time, right before going into battle.

The movies still reflect our manners. Gone, however, are the rules for violence. Violence was reserved for passion, grudges and ransom; now it's gratuitous and random.

Once we believed that "manners make the man" (and woman) and "a man (and woman) is betrayed by his (her) manners." Now, we seem to believe that "grunge" in every form makes the man or woman.

England was big on manners, inherited, no doubt, from the aristocracy who, in combination with Puritanism, passed them on to Americans. They have evolved because "to Americans, English manners are far more frightening than none at all" (from "Pictures From an Institution"). It seems we've gone from cool to bad, which is rad.

Graduation Retrospect

What a week it was. I attended a wedding, five graduations, shook 800 hands, listened to 20 speeches or so, had my 83rd birthday and fell off a curb.

All of which convinced me that we're giving the wrong graduation speeches and that, given a chance, I could give a really good talk next year. It won't be about believing in yourself, never giving up, or becoming competent, compassionate and communicative. In other words, it's time to give a speech not about qualities that lead to success, but the qualities that need to be eliminated in order to accomplish more than your parents.

One speaker, the Kelly Walsh valedictorian, did provide a large dollop of realism by telling his classmates about the difference between the possibilities and the probabilities of success, and it seemed timely to outline my proposed 2014 graduation speech.

During the wedding I attended, the minister talked a lot about "cleaving" and I think he meant sticking together and so I tried to push away the image of a meat cleaver. The important message is to warn the graduates that, although it's very important when marrying to stick to their mate, it's also very important to develop some skills and self-confidence because it's possible they'll have to either pay alimony or raise and support three kids by themselves. I would warn them that the word "cleave" isn't a derivative of cleavage.

I do think it's important to mention milestones, just like every other graduation speaker. I would emphasize, however, that it applies more to the parent than the graduate. They need to understand that parents are free at last ... maybe not financially, but morally, physically, mentally and legally. Grad, you're on your own and it's time to take stock not only of the distance you've traveled, but the quality of your journey.

Are you prepared? Did you know that your parents knew exactly what you were doing most of the time, but didn't know how to stop you? They're counting on those in charge to monitor your next stage of development. They're smiling because they're very grateful and even amazed that you survived long enough to walk across the stage, and that they'll moan about the empty nest, but secretly tingle with anticipation. Sure, they love you and in the name of love they've forgiven every darn-fool thing you ever did, and now it's your turn. Pride made them pretend you were perfect and they didn't think you'd believe that any more than you believed them when they told you that you'd learn more from your failures than your successes or that self-gratification gives you pimples.

Grads, they noticed when you stood in the middle of the soccer field looking at your iPad, or texting while the neighbor's kid scored. They gave you the ribbon and the praise because everyone told them that if they didn't they would scar your self-confidence for life. Admittedly, they're worried that you're going off to an expensive college already thinking you know everything there is to know, and maybe they shouldn't have helped you think more of yourself than the evidence warranted. So you'll survive when an employer fires you, because he doesn't care about whether you're confident you can do the job if you haven't done it. Your folks will probably let you come home when you're fired, but they've already turned your room into a library, so don't count on staying long.

I do have a comforting message for the grads that they probably missed while everyone was taking care of their sensitive egos. It's a simple message: up to half of your decisions will be mistakes, and that's not only human, but OK because learning's a lifelong activity.

One final point to convince everyone I'd make a good graduation speaker. I have a wealth of illustrations about mistakes and how important they are to us. Mistakes finally give one the chance to learn that life's about balancing confidence with competence, popularity with principle, heart with mind, modesty with ego, body with soul.

I'm just the person to confess to graduates that anyone who assured them that they have a birthright to think well of themselves is full of baloney. Confidence doesn't cause success; success results in confidence. One problem is that we confuse "success" with "value," and Graduate, you're valuable because you're a diamond disguised as a human — imperfect but possible of transcendence when polished. You'll grow out of the "me" stage, and accomplish the unexpected, the unthinkable and the remarkable.

So I'm available if anyone wants to listen to a lame 83-year-old who may fall off the stage, who admits she's been wrong 42 years, can't remember what the message is, but still cleaves to the idea that she can change the world one graduate at a time.

Relationships? Really?

Does there seem to be an inverse relationship between our talk about relationships and the absence or diminishment of them?

Is it possible that casual sex is really a relationship? Or that people listed on Facebook are really friends? Or that political promises become policy? Or that people who say they pity the poor actually behave as though they do?

What does this new mantra, "it's all about relationships," mean? Everywhere you turn, whether it's church, government, business or non-profits, we hear that if we focus on relationships we'll solve every problem and fulfill promised destinies.

If we mean that we must develop a more positive interaction among diverse peoples, save self-government and make peace in the world, I'm for it. We're all tired of division, conflict and inaction. But we have to do more than talk about "relationships" or view relationships as shallow interactions between or among people. Getting along and simply avoiding conflict won't do the trick.

Being agreeable doesn't take the place of creative conflict, spirited discussion, and the matching of values to make a decision. Getting along isn't a substitute for setting goals, respecting processes and taking action. Behavior needs to reflect values, and action needs to follow thoughtful consideration. Everything doesn't turn out right just because we get along or go along, any more than everything turns out right with constant conflict and division.

It's hard to recognize different perspectives and work together for solutions that don't violate our own long-held values and beliefs. That takes genuine, two-way communication.

Ah, but that's the rub. We've adopted a general mode of communication that engages a limited amount of thought and almost none of the senses. Do we really "communicate" if we can't hear, see, smell or touch the other person? Wouldn't it help to develop relationships if we knew whether the person uttering "OMG" was on his knees or using an obscene gesture?

It takes a fair amount of thought, along with the notion of the "common good" and the engagement of our senses to work with people. It seems like individualism in the name of freedom has supplanted the idea that we're in this together and need to agree on what we want to happen, as well as acceptable behaviors. We'll have to convince ourselves of the necessity of work to achieve the best for more than just ourselves.

When did freedom mean going through stop signs and believing that we had no obligations to other people, including children? We lose the sense of community when we accept the idea that some humans deserve spectacular wealth and others deserve to be without housing, food and dignity.

Did we decide that intimacy was simply a bodily function? Or that friendships were networks of those who could give us advantages of some kind? When did commitment turn into convenience? Did this happen gradually, or was it caused by something in the stars?

Surely all this talk about relationships doesn't mean communications without contact, thinking without action, values without behavior, work without dignity, freedom without responsibility, conception without parenting. Surely what we viewed as a middle-class culture isn't gone, and we don't have to be puritans to maintain it.

Here's a revolutionary thought: maybe we should learn how to cooperate with a whole lot of people we don't like at all ... people we neither have a relationship with nor with whom we want a relationship.

If it's contemporary to believe that "everything is relationships," I hope it includes the relationships between the abstract and the concrete as well as mind and body, children and adults, people and nature. Otherwise, we might just as well say, "It's not what you know, it's who you know," and forget the finer nuances of relationships.

Fortunately, I believe in cycles, and if relationships are a little weak at the moment, they'll return. In the meantime, we could talk less of relationships and more about organizing to do a complex amount of work with a variety of people, with or without relationships.

Charity or Entitlement?

There seems to be a consensus among those over 50 that the trouble with this generation is they feel they're entitled.

The rest of us seem to be of two minds on the subject. On the one hand, we believe everyone should have the basics such as food and water, housing and clothing. On the other, we disdain and resent people who act as though they're entitled, without effort, to these things and more.

There's a difference in the language. "Charity" is a noun and means voluntarily helping those in need as well as a tolerance in judging others, and "entitle" is a verb that gives someone permission, authorization or qualifications to do or receive something.

When the word entitle turned into the noun entitlement, the philosophy, as well as the grammar, changed radically. There's a big gap between my willingness to give and your claim that because of entitlement, I must do so.

It's easy to understand, politics withstanding, why many Americans resent others who claim assistance (entitlement) by entitling themselves. Maybe those who feel that way don't see it as a vulgarization of the language, but a corruption of their values.

Perhaps the shift is related to the seemingly new definition of freedom as an unlimited right. Or maybe people feel that since you're a human being and they're human beings, you're obliged to help them survive.

Without understanding and sympathy toward those who could work, but can't for a variety of reasons including weak job skills, no available jobs, no place to leave children, etc., neither charity nor entitlement solve the problem.

Several non-profits seem to bridge the gap between the noun and the verb. Many help, but several outline conditions. Among them are Seton House, which not only provides housing, but spells out expectations about behavior and how to become self-sufficient. Joshua's Storehouse is another agency that not only provides food to families every week, but promotes volunteerism and a sense of community and working together, as well.

The Central Wyoming Rescue Mission expects behavior changes, and Habitat for Humanity helps people build their own homes. There are a wealth of non-profits providing people not only charity, but a chance to change their lives.

These non-profits give people faith in themselves, and they begin to hope that with a change in attitude, habits, skills, education and a sense of community, they can take charge of their own lives.

Non-profits demonstrate every day that charity alone won't solve the problem of human need, nor will entitlement achieved without effort. The agencies that invest in human development give people the tools they need to take care of themselves and with that, the self-respect that comes with self-sufficiency.

Too bad we, collectively (government), don't get the picture. Many non-profits have blended the notions of charity and entitlement because they understand that each, separately, spells dependency.

The Dog Ate My Homework

Why is it that when I'm explaining why something happened, it sounds like an explanation rather than an excuse, and when someone else is explaining why something happened, it sounds more like an excuse than an explanation?

Educators, school boards, legislators and other elected officials have searched for years for the answer to why students are dropping out of school before graduating, and why they're not prepared when they do graduate for further training or college.

We've all used "the dog ate my homework excuse" on occasion, but it seems to me the habit's getting all too prevalent. Students say they dropped out because they were bored, when the real problem was that because of poverty, discrimination, violence at home or anxiety, they couldn't concentrate.

In education, the elected officials at the national and state levels point to the teacher or the school and decide that the drop-out problem and knowledge and skill level of the graduates lies with them. They think they have solutions called "accountability systems" that they themselves don't have, but that can be applied to teachers, schools and districts. Never mind that students are distracted by cars, technology and sex and grow up in an anything-goes culture. We can't blame students for being undisciplined when the norm is freedom without responsibility.

If we can simply blame teachers and tell them to shape up or we'll wipe out the public school system and install private enterprise, we don't have to deal with complex issues such as how to build curriculum and instruction based on what we know, such as: a) all children don't have similar brains; b) all children don't learn on the same time schedule; c) the habits in the home are relevant to the willingness and ability to learn; d) the community culture and expectations influence the school goals; and e) learning is controlled by the learner, not the teacher.

In other words, if policy makers believe that the teaching-learning transaction consists of the adult pouring in the right information and the student vomiting it back, and we then measure the level of the regurgitation, there will be no changes in the results. Everything educators know about how to motivate, inspire and engage students will be subverted by testing and accountability systems based on the facts-in, vomit-out theory.

Educators are prepared to be accountable; they just wish that those in charge would base accountability on a better knowledge of what they do, not as information givers but as facilitators of a process that puts students in the center and helps them become responsible for their own learning.

The drop-out problem or preparing graduates for employment or further education isn't going to be solved by holding teachers, schools or districts accountable until it's clear what they're accountable for. That isn't possible until there's a better understanding of how children, or adults, learn. Blaming teachers is a little like blaming the fire-fighters for starting the fire.

I have this strange thought that we need to slow down the well-intended national and state efforts to fix education, and instead ask them to be clear about what they expect students to know and be able to do, and then leave it up to those on the firing line (teachers, principals and other educators) to do it. Deadlines are acceptable, and accountability is expected.

What local districts have gotten from the national and state policy-makers are unrealistic goals, the application of punishment instead of support, incorrect measurements and burdensome reports that divert teachers and students from learning important skills and knowledge that could be applied to life and work. Teachers have been forced to teach to the test, rather than test what has been learned. Then teachers and students have been judged by the test that measured information retention rather than thinking, and recall rather than problem-solving.

But there's more to the story. Slowly, non-educators have redefined education to mean the process by which we make people employable. Gone is the Jeffersonian notion that education is essential to self-government. At the present pace, the young will be totally ignorant about their own and other cultures and language, their political heritage and economic systems. Teachers have to struggle to find time to encourage and facilitate a system of critical thinking, innovation, creativity and the marriage of knowledge and skills.

Many educators have solutions based on what they know about learning, but sometimes the policy-makers seem to send the dogs out to eat our homework.

Get On With It

Editor's note: In this column, I refer to legislation in which the constitutional office of State Superintendent of Schools was replaced by a governor-appointed Director of Education. The bill was found unconstitutional and was an attempt to replace a superintendent that legislators didn't like or thought was incompetent.

It's surprising, no, disgusting that the Legislature hangs on to the Hill Bill like a dog that hasn't been fed enough yet. Why haven't they come up with the simple legal solution to the dilemma they created? Why not spend the months until the next election preparing a constitutional amendment that asks the people whether they wish: a) to continue to elect a state superintendent; b) to elect a State Board of Education that then appoints a state superintendent; or c) to elect a governor who appoints a Director of Education.

Why are they still obsessing about Superintendent Hill, and for that matter, why do they think that outlining the state superintendent's duties means doing more than spelling out generally the superintendent's responsibilities in meeting their expectations for the students statewide?

The legislators who get it in their heads that they're totally in charge of education are disregarding the peoples' rights and desires, local control and the separation of powers.

In addition to a violation of the separation of powers, they've also disregarded a long-held and cherished concept of local control of the schools. It's the greatest irony that the legislature is deciding who's competent. It's the greatest travesty that they've disregarded and disrespected attempts by other governors, superintendents and professional experts to establish nationwide standards to upgrade the performance of all students.

These standards establish high expectations (that can be measured), not curriculum, and certainly not instruction. This is the UNITED States of America, and this legislature's acting like Wyoming's a separate country, isolated from the states we united with beginning more than 200 years ago. Sometimes, it appears that we're ignoring the hard battle 13 different colonies went through to establish a united states and agree upon a constitution that recognized individual states, and confirmed the responsibilities and powers of all states, united.

In other words, the Cindy Hill matter is bigger than the individual some legislators have attacked as incompetent (another irony). This legislature has challenged the right of the majority of people to elect their officials, and then they've challenged the court's decision and are now unwilling to let a duly-elected official fulfill her obligations to oversee education in the state and administer the Department of Education.

It's very sad that the legislature has done this with the full cooperation, if not instigation, of the governor through his instructions to the attorney general. When the highest executive official doesn't defend the separation of powers, but joins the legislative branch in violating the constitution, the citizens should rise up in indignation and action. Certainly the question of whether a little power corrupts and complete power corrupts completely, is in order.

Will the voters, ranging from Tea Party and Liberty Party Constitutionalists to the liberal wing of the Democratic party, speak up at election time so that those involved in the Hill Bill understand the seriousness of what they've done? Or will the legislature come to a new understanding now, and correct their error immediately?

Now's the time to get on with it.

Holding a Grudge

I suppose it makes sense to hold a grudge. If someone does something despicable, we suppose we ought to remember it, but the problem is that we have to "hold" a grudge and it's this "holding" that seems to divert us from the fulfilling things in life.

I decided I'd rather be a grudgee than a grudgeor, once I decided that forgetting was almost as good as forgiving. Once you forget what you did or was done to you, it can no longer be counted as a grudge. Grudges are, by nature, long-lasting resentments.

Personally, when someone seems to be holding a grudge about me, I not only can't remember what it was, but I hope neither can they. If they still don't treat me nicely, it means there's something about me that's repugnant to them. Truthfully, I'd rather someone resent me for something I said or did than treat me unkindly for some other reason, such as I'm just not likeable.

That means I can feel sorry for someone who holds a grudge because he/she has to think of it every day, hold it close and nurse it. I can ignore someone whose view of life and the world is focused and flat.

A few years ago, I took a job with a person who lied to me four years previously for the simple reason that I forgot he lied. I assume he forgot, too, or decided to pretend he did.

It was then I decided that if I held a grudge, I would only hold it for a day or two and then forget it. What a relief to discover an unintended consequence of this decision was that it was now possible to make the same mistake twice. Most of us hate repeating ourselves, but understand that self-righteousness is the reward for not making mistakes over and over again. Besides, it's always possible to give an old mistake a new twist so that we can conclude that we've made a variety of mistakes.

So if grudge-holding or spirit-dampening, I think I've found a formula for limiting or even curing the habit. First, forget to practice resentment since holding a grudge is a long-standing resentment and can't be held without practice. Second, don't write anything down. Don't keep a journal, and don't write anything but appointments in a daytimer or a calendar. If you can't live without writing, jot things down on a slip of paper that can't be located later. Or write things on the wrong page, the wrong date, the wrong month. For example, you could note that someone was nasty, but you don't write the date, the name or the grievance. When you find the note, you can throw it away immediately. Third, when something unpleasant is happening, let your mind lose its focus by imagining that you're at a banquet full of people who are here just to honor you. That will prevent resentments every time. Fourth, never be anything but polite to a person for whom you should hold a grudge, or who seems to have one about you. Excessive politeness or solicitation usually means you don't want to get close to them. It's a kind of noblesse oblige. Fifth, it helps to have some hearing loss because it's impossible to remember something, even an offense, if you didn't hear it in the first place. This is the one practice you can fake, but pretending works best if you're under 21 or over 70.

Finally, confront the person who "wronged" you so that you know why they resents you, but be prepared for either an incident you forgot or a litany of your faults. It also works if you're the grudgeor; tell the grudgee, but understand that it's hard to hold the grudge if you talk to the grudgee.

Please feel free to use the list. It's almost fool-proof, and not only that, you can ignore the old axiom, "The past is prologue to the future."

Is It the Guns or the Values?

Editor's note: The Wyoming legislature has considered allowing concealed weapons in schools, the University of Wyoming and other public places several times over the years. Wyoming has extensive freedom to carry weapons, but the so-called gun advocates wish to expand it and any objection is considered "gun grabbing."

It would appear that HB114 is about safety, but is it? Or perhaps it's about freedom, but is it? Is the bill to cement the right to bear arms? Perhaps, but at the price of free (safe) assembly, free speech and a free press? I know we love guns, but does extending concealed weapon carrying really represent the "Wyoming Way"?

Or is HB114 a classic example of a bill that plants a garden of unintended consequences? What if it's based on several false assumptions?

Assumption 1: That "they" are out to "grab" our guns and that we must, therefore, arm everyone in every place at all times. Is this bill more about viewing both the national and local government as the enemy, or any government as the enemy? And is there a word for that?

Assumption 2: That people are divided into two categories and only two categories: the "good guys" and the "bad guys." We're Mother Teresa or Osama Bin Laden. Do you know anyone who's one-dimensional? Who's always kind, considerate, "law-abiding" and never loses their temper? Or anyone who's always unkind, discourteous, cruel, dishonest and violent? In other words, good people do bad things, and I suppose bad people do good things. After all, Clyde loved Bonnie, but hated bankers.

Assumption 3: That "bad" people plan attacks on those who can't defend themselves because they're unarmed. Well, bad people could be logical, but if people who kill other people are emotionally or mentally defective, they probably aren't capable of planning ahead. They also have a tendency to either kill themselves or commit suicide by police.

Assumption 4: That the communities in Wyoming are likely to be attacked because they live in a place where there are no other options to keep themselves safe. The odds that children will go to bed hungry, be physically or sexually abused, or have none of the enriching, educational experiences that will keep them safe now or in the future are much more likely than the odds of being attacked by violent strangers who have targeted them because they think no one is equipped to defend them.

Assumption 5: That the local individuals and agencies don't have or won't plan other ways to keep their citizens safe or that the state doesn't trust them to do so.

Assumption 6: That the bill strengthens the Bill of Rights. But freedom of religion, freedom of speech, freedom of assembly and freedom of the press could be compromised if everyone decided to carry concealed weapons. And does the freedom to be armed have no limitations about where and when and why?

Since arming people with concealed weapons could radically alter the kind of society we live in, shouldn't we question the values reflected in HB114?

When we carry a concealed weapon, don't we assume that everyone we meet is a potential enemy rather than a potential friend? And if we assume that everyone we meet views us this way too, doesn't it affect our behavior as well as our entire outlook on life?

What other assumptions underlie HB114? Does the state not trust local law enforcement, school boards, city councils, county commissioners, parents or merchants within a community to install a variety of ways to keep people safe? We all live at the local level and is there any difference between whether the state or the federal government assume they have to make decisions that should be left locally?

I wonder if there's a yearning to turn back the clock to the Wyoming of yesteryear. Guns were carried a long time ago, but they were visible and they were checked at the door to public places. There was little law and less order. But there was more than range wars. There was self-reliance and cooperation, independence and neighborliness, and a live-and-let-live philosophy.

If I arm myself because I don't know whether everyone else is armed and I need to defend myself, will I hesitate long enough to be sure I'm being threatened, or will I act too hastily to be able to justify hurting another human being?

Have we asked ourselves what happens to the quality of our lives and our moral fiber if HB114 passes? I don't think we favor trading four freedoms for one, nor order for chaos. I trust that Wyoming's way is to balance individuality with community, cooperation with independence, and freedom with responsibility.

Keep History

I've always loved history; in fact, my undergraduate studies were of literature and history because it seemed to me that history tells what happened, and sometimes it leaves it up to our imaginations or literature to figure out why.

I love the artifacts of history, especially old houses, old cars, old books, old records. One can weave stories from the artifacts. Take old houses, for instance. When you tour the historic Bishop House, don't you feel the presence of the lives that once permeated the place?

I owned, well, occupied, an old house on Central Avenue near the capitol in Cheyenne, which my daughter, grandson and neighbor claimed was haunted. Whether ghosts actually turned on the record player, rang the doorbell or walked across the dining room at night, I don't know since I was dealing with real people who called at midnight to threaten me with car bombs.

I did feel the lifestyle of a century of occupants in the old house in Cheyenne, and in Minneapolis, and in Casper. The tie-hacks were in the walls at the Twin Pines Motel I once owned in Dubois.

I was delighted to read about all the downtown buildings in Casper that are on the historic register and of the possibility that a dozen more may qualify. My attitude is save them all. This is our history.

The criteria used by the historic preservationists works well for old buildings and sites, but being 50 years old, still looking like they originally looked and having historic significance doesn't exactly apply to old love letters, tennis rackets and old tea strainers ... unless very loosely applied.

What criteria do we apply to saving our personal stuff? One can't just save things that make us look good, like old photos or newspaper articles. If they're really historical, researchers will search for the unflattering, truthful items, according to Gibbons, who said that "History is little more than a register of the crimes, follies, misfortune of mankind."

That may influence the artifacts we save in a community but it surely isn't what fills our personal closets, attics and garages. We save our compliments, our awards, our accomplishments and, yes, our follies. Mostly, we save our sentiments.

That's why the first buildings we save are our Victorian mansions, and we're fortunate that some foresighted officials also saved buildings like Fire Station #1 on David Street, the Casper Motor Company on Yellowstone, Natrona County High School, St. Anthony's Church, the Midwest and Ohio Oil Company buildings, the Odd Fellows and the Elks and, of course, Fort Caspar. Many times, they serve a different purpose, but they look like they did 50-100 years ago, and they have historic significance.

There may be a dozen or more buildings that could be placed on the historic register and a half-dozen neighborhoods, according to the Preservation Solution Study. I hope they are because I regret that two of the first schools in Casper were demolished and there are two more — the School for the Deaf and Roosevelt (old North Casper) — whose fates may still be in jeopardy. I hope the Council also takes a look at Sherrie's Place; it may have housed more than food in it's early Sand Bar years!

Collectively, we've always had to balance progress with preservation, and perhaps that's true on the personal level. Are these old cross-cut saws, shaving mugs, glass marbles, catcher's gloves, old insurance policies and school board minutes part of history or relics of our hysteria?

I say let your children sort through them and decide. It's the least they can do for all the junk you stored for them during their early years and travels. But on a community level, let's abide by the criteria established by the National Register for Historic Places and designate even more downtown buildings, including Sherrie's Place, as historic.

In Defense of a Closed Mind

The mark, they tell me, of a tolerant, kind, understanding person is an open mind. The admonishment to "keep an open mind" is a kindly way of saying don't be old, bigoted, ill-informed, biased and wrong.

Most of us have large areas of the brain that have been closed for years and need someone to remind us to pry it open periodically. On the other hand, if left open constantly, the wind will surely blow everything out of it, including life's memories and lessons. Weren't we given different parts of the brain so that we could we trap information, lessons and passions in order to use them again?

If we decide not to be afraid of closing our minds, we discover that the whole idea of keeping or getting an open mind is overrated. We have to remember that we're in windy Wyoming and it doesn't take much to blow everything in an open mind over to Nebraska or beyond. It's just as logical to hang on to our thoughts as it is to hang on to our hats, especially our Stetsons.

Mind you, it's probably both logical and appropriate to consider new ideas and to simply find out why someone holds a very strange, exotic idea that seems to defy fact or logic, but that's not the same as keeping an open mind that's blown about by whatever is heard, seen, touched or smelled.

In fact, there ought to be a time limit on how long a mind can stay open. Shouldn't there be a certain point where the mind decides what it believes and therefore, what it thinks? Isn't that why we're provided with experiences and schooling?

Should we be ashamed to admit that we've closed our minds to cohabitation without marriage, or birthing without established patrimony/matrimony? Should we open our minds to the possibility that another race is inferior, or that anyone who's different from ourselves isn't entitled to the same rights we have? Shall we consider thinking that alcohol and other drugs are good for us? Are we supposed to accept the idea that running red lights, squeezing in front of another driver or giving him the finger is appropriate behavior?

If experience has taught us that dipping our chips in the common bowl spreads germs, should we be tolerant about it? If we really believe that a higher minimum wage would be good for business, should we be open to the argument that poverty is always with us?

Should we be open-minded about whether men should make more money for the same work that women do? Should we remain open-minded about whether children who live in poverty are entitled to the same educational opportunity as the education we designed for middle-class children?

Is it possible that asking someone to keep an open mind is the same as asking someone to demonstrate that they're not bigoted, afraid of new ideas or just plain old? If we really mean to cut off a discussion about a specific action or idea, why do we disguise it by calling it an "open" mind?

When is the right time to say, "No, I refuse to open my mind to that possibility"? It seems to me, the right time is when we're old enough or experienced enough, have faith enough or hope enough to be unafraid of having someone imply that if we won't consider anything and everything, we're not only closed-minded, but bigoted, biased, intolerant and out of step with the modern world.

Admittedly, we risk the hazard of cob webs if we never open up to new ideas, actions or adventures, and there are too many examples of people (other people) having the answer before they've heard the question.

There's some truth to the saying that "Minds are like parachutes … they only function when they're open" (Don Juan). But there's something to be said about minds as steel traps, especially when they've captured what we hold dear and true.

Perhaps the mind needs to be open to the question, but is encouraged to close upon what experience, education and values indicates is the answer?

One thing is surely true: "No passion so effectively robs the mind of all its powers of acting and reasons as fear," especially the fear of appearing closed-minded.

Noblesse Oblige, Civility, Charity

Though I've been in Wyoming more than 50 years, I had never heard the expression "heal up and hair over" until I read the latest Wyoming Humanities Council booklet by the same name. For the past few years, they've programmed around the theme of civility, and the ranch expression is a term for the animal healing process. In human terms, it means "get over it."

It seems to me that the farmers and ranchers live their lives getting over it. They overcome the weather, the market, the bucking bronco, invasive hunters and downed fences, and they not only get over it, they manage to be polite.

I wondered why. What, I asked myself, is the difference between those early aristocratic Americans and contemporary patriots? What would it take to regain some of the intelligence and civility the Founding Fathers demonstrated? How do we heal up and hair over?

How do we change a world that keeps wounding itself and never seems to take the steps needed for a healing process? Maybe we could use a homemaker's trick by starting in the middle and nibbling our way out. Or maybe we could do what most bureaucrats do and make a list. Or maybe we could just make a list because once we get to the forgetful stage, we need to remind ourselves of what we intended and reward ourselves by checking items off, one by one.

What if we decided we'd restore a pleasant, productive, problem-solving world by taking the following steps? First, we would all practice noblesse oblige. That means we would all be helpful to everyone else because of our own good fortune. In America, of course, we earned our good fortune rather than inherited it, didn't we? Think of the impact on everyday life: we'd stop at red lights, take turns at intersections, let others cut in, say hello to neighbors and help old ladies cross the street whether they wanted you to or not. The possibilities at the lowest level could create a better mood for the really big things.

Second, we could be charitable. We could read I Corinthians for a broader definition of charity and start treating others kindly. We could remind ourselves that even though we're smart, patient, modest and righteous, it means nothing if our motives are lousy. We could contemplate what we become as sounding brass and tinkling symbols, or in modern terms, how being full of ourselves may have contributed to the condition we're in.

Once we accept charity as a necessary condition for healing over, we could give up the notion that the poor are responsible for their poverty, that teachers are responsible for student learning and that doctors are responsible for death.

The third step is civility. Clearly, civility isn't passive acceptance of any idea or value, but it's respecting the other person's views. It really isn't impossible to discuss two oppositional ideas and come up with a third that's acceptable to both sides. But it takes strength of character (which we've already attained in step two), and the capability to doubt ourselves and others. Those we admired, such as Jefferson, Franklin or Emerson, concerned themselves with the issue.

Problems aren't solved by viewing other people as evil or from another species, and we seem to do that a lot lately. Whole nations act as though they're fighting interplanetary wars with aliens. If we think we're that different, it helps to be charitable, civil and polite.

I received a survey last week from the head of Wyoming Gun Owners who wants funds to fight anyone of either party who wants to control guns. He calls us gun grabbers. I could have been angry, but noblesse oblige works when the individual calling you names is more to be pitied than censured. The rear window sign in Wyoming pickups that says "Welcome to Wyoming. Consider us all armed" could reflect more of us if they added "with charity, civility and charm."

Finally, the fourth step to heal and hair over is to develop good manners. Again, ranchers and cowboys seem to lead the way. Last week one called me ma'am so many times I was beginning to feel precious. Nothing signals class more than manners. If you go to restaurants, you immediately identify who has the table manners you were taught and who doesn't, but the real test of good manners is whether we can be charitable and civil to those with whom we disagree. It's opening the door to the mind, not the restaurant, that matters.

When civility, charity, manners and noblesse oblige are available to the whole world, why aren't there more takers?

Arts and Humanities: Basic to Community

During a period when the whole world seems to distrust other individuals, ideas, institutions and countries, the U.S. president is proposing a budget that adds to our ability to kill each other and cuts our ability to build civility and creativity.

The arts, humanities and public broadcasting have been cut or eliminated in the budget being proposed to Congress. The message is clear: human beings are grossly self-interested and bent on destroying efforts that appeal to and enhance the qualities that differentiate us from other living creatures.

Worry about the economy and security are valid concerns, but we are more than robots that are programmed to keep ourselves safe in order to produce "things."

Wyoming has long valued the arts and humanities, but we can't sustain support of either without help from the federal and state governments. The state is too small to support both with private donations alone. Without public support, there would be little or no statuary that tells strangers and citizens alike that Casper values the arts.

Almost every town in Wyoming has a music community that enlivens and entertains with sounds ranging from banjo and guitar to symphonic violins and cellos. The Wyoming Humanities Council has provided small and large communities with storytelling, public television documentaries, discussion programs on public policy issues and civility.

The point is that we don't live by bread alone. We're creatures that need to understand why we think and act as we do. We desire engagement in activities that raise us above the base instincts of survival. We need art, both performing and visual, and the humanities, both theoretical and practical.

Cuts in the national budget will severely affect the public humanities and arts program in Wyoming at the same time as millions of dollars are cut from K-12 and higher education. Often, the first things cut are music and art programs in public schools, and philosophy and literature courses at the college level. We're inclined to focus on job/career preparation and economic development above all else.

At the very time that we need to experience problem-solving, creativity, civility and cooperation, we seem to be turning to expenditures that promote self-interest and divisiveness. The humanities and arts aren't simply studies having little to do with everyday life. The humanities demonstrate and teach the kinds of skills needed to separate the truth from fiction, the relationships between ideas, action and consequences, and how to transcend our baser natures. The skills of exploration, synthesis, analysis and problem-solving are mobile skills that can be applied to all areas of everyday life.

Together, Wyomingites must convince Congressional members and legislators that there are more guidelines to budgeting than simply cutting costs and government. Whether in government or personally, money should never be a goal, but a tool used judiciously to reflect our values ... as human beings, citizens in a democratic country and members of a global family.

Most of all, we need the arts and humanities. They're vehicles for wisdom and beauty ... and perhaps even character and morality. They're important to democracy because they speak to equality, fairness, innovation, creativity, justice and freedom. All fail in practice if the common values aren't foundational.

Oddly enough, the arts and humanities are also good economics: art gives good first impressions, music draws crowds, and our programs about issues gather people together to help build community and avoid the necessity to prepare for divisiveness and war.

Good Losers and Sour Grapes

You may have wondered where I've been, and then again, with a generally hectic past four months, you may not have noticed I wasn't there since hardly anybody seemed to be all there.

But just in case you missed me, I'm glad to say I've returned from what has been termed "running for the legislature." Why it's called "running" when it consists of walking hundreds of miles is unclear.

Also unclear is why people ask if we feel badly because we "lost." No one says "you lost the job" after you applied but didn't get hired, so why do they call it "losing an election"?

There's a big difference between losing than simply not getting the job. We always think we're the best qualified, but the boss decides, and in elections, the people are boss.

There can be three different results from the concept of losing. One can feel as though they shouldn't have lost (and risk being called poor losers); they can claim they didn't really care whether they won (and be suspected of eating sour grapes); or they can be angry and put a hex on the person elected so he/she can't do the job.

My friends are particularly anxious that I don't look like a poor loser. Since I don't look at running for office and not being hired as losing something I never had, I didn't lose and I'm no poorer for it. On the other hand, if those of us not elected are relieved, we face another hazard: looking like sour grapes.

So in an effort to clarify this whole subject of winning and losing, let's settle for the fact that those of us who were outnumbered two-to-one never really expected to be elected. Yet we gave it the same, or more, effort than those who were elected. It's a bit like applying for a job that you didn't think you'd get, but gave it your best shot.

Suppose that it's possible to be a good loser and a poor winner? We don't really deserve sympathy, but want to be praised for the effort. What makes a person a good loser? Well, for starters, we don't have to move to Cheyenne for two months and that means we don't have to find a house sitter and animal caretakers. It means we don't have to work with a bunch of people we would normally find annoying.

We don't have to figure out how to pass Medicaid expansion and preserve public lands or how to narrow the wage disparity while cutting budgets, services and jobs.

I suppose it does sound like sour grapes when I say the unelected can sit by the fireplace and read the books they started four months ago. Personally, I have even more material for my memoir called "Catching Spears in Wyoming." We can all go to coffees, lunches, plays and concerts, and visit children in warmer places.

We can finally take walks up the 11th Street hill just like Jane and Mike Sullivan without stopping to catch our breath since we're in shape from door-to-door walking. We're even more eager to talk to strangers in the grocery store or doctor's office since we learned that Wyomingites are really nice even when they don't intend to endorse you.

Isn't it the cowboy code to claim that it isn't whether you win or lose, but how you play the game? I'd say those of us who tried but didn't get the job would neither regret applying nor want to repeat it soon, so don't cry for us. Sometimes we're fortunate we didn't get the job ... and that's not sour grapes.

Talking With Your Hands

In spite of the crude references to hands lately, and our annoyance with candidates who keep pointing at us, I respect and admire the hands. They tell us things in an honest way, while the words coming from the mouth are often unreliable.

There's a reason why the majority of references to hands are in the Bible. We commend our spirits into the hands; we join hands in matrimony; we lay violent hands upon ourselves; we clasp the right hands of fellowship; we're told to strengthen weak hands, and are warned that temples aren't built with hands.

Values are transmitted through hands. It may have changed the history of the world if the Nazi salute had been with palms upward. The cupped hands receive communion; open hands ask for understanding.

It means something to extend the hand of fellowship across the ocean. Clearly, no one's reach is that long, but it's fraught with symbolism. We spit on the hands to prepare them for hard work. We don't spit on the hands just before eating or in preparation for a handshake. We clap them in approval and pound them in fury.

Have you noticed that when a person is embarrassed or they feel like crying, they place their hands over their face, and when they laugh when they shouldn't, they place their hands over their mouth? Why do babies laugh when we cover our eyes with our hands and say "boo" when we remove them?

Is there any question about our loving intents when we use both hands to cradle a small animal? Or make a fist when we're angry? Hands speak. What do they say when you cross your arms and tuck both hands under the opposite arm? I suppose it could mean that you can't think of what to do with cracking fingernails, but it probably means you're not really engaged in this boring conversation. Maybe we just don't want someone to look at our chests, or maybe our hands are cold. Personally, I think it's more appropriate to put on gloves or place my hands in my pockets if they're cold.

Does the habit of bumping fists nowadays to indicate agreement bother you at all? Fists usually mean we're ready to fight, so how did we adopt a supposedly warm gesture that's like bathing with your clothes on? We learn a lot by placing our palms on another's palms and wrapping our fingers around another's hand, so why have we substituted fist bumps?

Sure, hands can be used to push away as well as draw another person near, and fingers can be used to braid another's fingers or used to insult. Hands tell you things: calloused hands mean someone works hard at physical labor, while soft hands with a knob on the index finger used to indicate a desk job with a lot of writing. Now, we can't identify carpel tunnel just by looking and conclude that someone sits at a computer all day.

Hands are meant to hold books, and fingers are meant to flip pages. And we wash our hands of people we don't agree with, but dig them in the dirt to get close to nature. The thumb was once used to get a ride from strangers whom we trusted, but is now used to send endless, often shallow messages on a machine that will do anything you ask.

We fold our hands over our hearts to say thank you; we also use them to pick pockets, punch, shame, accuse and damn, as well as for knitting friendships, welcoming others, helping our neighbors, cleaning up, building, drawing and playing a musical instrument.

No matter how much plastic surgery keeps the face unwrinkled or how much dye keeps the hair colored, the hands tell us how old someone is every time. When your grandchild can lift the skin on the back of your hand and it stays suspended, it's impossible to lie about your age. But this hand can still curl around a hot cup of tea or coffee, pat a child's head, or wave at a neighbor.

When the hands can no longer hold a pen, strike the keys on a computer, hold a fork or cut some meat, it can still hold a cane for balance and hold another's hand in pain or pleasure. If the intentions are bad, we can always warn people away by telling them to keep their hands off.

Hands separate us from most animals. Tigers and lions and bears rarely offer a clenched fist to bump. They don't hold their foreheads when they're perplexed, and they don't lend a hand in help. I have squirrels that finger-snatch peanuts, but they seem to communicate more with their tails than their hands … or so it seems.

I'd like to think that we're human not because we stand upright, but because we have hands and can work with them, pray with them, draw people close with them, paint a picture, play a violin, rob banks, hold guns, push, shove and hit. Animals don't do any of those things.

It's mostly people who have hands, and only they talk with them. That's my observation, and that means that the only hands that can save the world are ours. Touching with words is much colder than touching with hands and that's why "I just wanna hold your hand."

Needed or Needy?

I have begun to wonder whether the world is divided into two types of people: those who are needed and those who are needy. Most of us don't want to be needy, can't help it and view it as temporary. Those who get used to being needy sometimes begin to think they deserve the services of others. It must affect a person adversely to be needy because either consciously or not, they've accepted themselves as victims, if only temporarily.

Oddly enough, those who want to be needed may also become victims if those around them either don't appreciate what they have to offer, or have decided they no longer have anything to offer. We're told that it's an American cultural belief that people over 60 or so don't have anything to offer.

Older Americans' values, customs and skills seem to be obsolete. After over 40 years of organizing, supervising, budgeting, fundraising, training, policy-making and accomplishing goals, many of my friends and I feel unneeded and invisible. Some of us accept this as an invitation to be self-indulgent (which we were trained never to be), and some of us are really mad.

Since we're still geared to being helpful, we have to find someplace that still wants and needs our help and this usually means turning to the non-profits. We direct our efforts to hospice, nursing homes, American Cancer Society, and organizations for the blind, deaf, disabled and poor. They seem to appreciate and use our skills unless, of course, they're managed by those who assumed leadership in order to get ahead in the world. They may not want our advice or our skills. There are few of those in Casper, but if their ambitions focus on children, hardly anyone under 60 ever catches on.

I visited a nursing home three times a week for over three years, and when I no longer had a personal reason for doing so, I discovered that I missed it because I felt needed, wanted and appreciated. I shall probably volunteer again, but it will be painful when my loved one is no longer in residence.

It seems to me that there's an assumption that mostly what the older generation needs is health care, rides to the grocery store and doctors' offices, transportation and household chores. On close observation, I find that those are peripheral benefits and what they really need is to be needed. In conversations with the directors of senior centers, I discovered that the successful centers have a large membership involved in activities ranging from eating to dancing, lectures to games, forming new friendships and helping others. They're not the centers that assume that foot baths and health clinics sum up their lives; they're the centers that find out what skills and knowledge the seniors have and get them to share them with others, both their own age and children.

Children seem to appreciate the experiences of older people more than those who ought to know enough to do so. And the association with children keeps seniors vital and interested in the world around them. Children love being read to, and seniors love doing it. Children love to teach their grandparents how to use the computer, and seniors welcome the help and are amazed at the mysteries understood by those decades younger than them.

Some don't choose to be needy about physical things, but they do choose to be needed. They offer experiences and knowledge that sometimes threatens those who want to get ahead by keeping people needy.

Here's A Tip

This wind blows my mind ... figuratively and literally. I read a lot, and with the weather as lousy as it's been, I'm reading too much ... and now I've begun to think about ethereal things. During coffee, some friends initiated a discussion about tipping and wondered, among other things, whether the owner of an establishment should be tipped.

Now I'm haunted by these words that keep repeating themselves: "To tip or not to tip. That is the question: whether it is nobler to demonstrate our generosity or to appear to be a cheapskate."

The question diverted me from my concern about what was going to happen to public lands and medical care, and since no one takes my advice anyway, I decided to come up with a definitive answer to the question of tipping.

When do we tip? Whom do we tip? It could be insulting to tip the wrong person, and it could be dangerous to not tip the one who expects it. At the top of the list are servers. They not only expect to be tipped, but their managers give you a handy chart telling you how much. And they should since they have to think of some way to make up for the shortfall they pay in wages.

The whole idea began with a small reward for personal services. So does that mean the person who carries our luggage and the one who cleans our house? Do we include the person who shovels the walk, and if they're under age, can we tip them less than the grown guy that pledged to help little old ladies?

Do we tip if the service is mediocre or unsatisfactory? Is tipping an act of generosity, a donation, a handout, a reward or a bonus for extra service? Is it a symbol of our kindness or of our wealth? If we give because it's expected and we have to, are we endorsing the "entitlement age"?

The big question is whether we're supporting the employer or the employee. What does a person's wages cover? Is a waitress paid to deliver the food, or does the patron pay for food and the delivery? If we aren't paying for the delivery, how come every restaurant isn't simply a serve-yourself buffet?

If we tip the snow shoveler, is it because he removed all the snow and deserves a reward, or because if we don't, he'll kick some of the stuff back on the sidewalk? If we tip the people who trim the trees, is it because they charged less than the company with the cherry picker and insurance, or because they made the tree look better than you expected?

The hardest question of all is whether we reward only for services that go beyond what's expected by the customer. If we tip, does it mean we didn't expect as much as the next person? Do we pay a little more for reputation than for extra services? If the business owner also attends our church, should we indicate that we're charitable by giving a little extra? Can tipping be viewed as a way of indicating that there is a class system and those of us who can pay for services can also be generous with the servants?

I tried to find a history of tipping after I determined that I was incapable of writing a handbook for my friend, but I didn't find one. The practice began long ago, ever since some people expected other people to do for them what they didn't want to — or couldn't — do for themselves. Come to think of it, that was the reason we formed governments, too ... though I doubt taxes are viewed as a reward for services, even though they ought to be.

Anyway, it looks like one of the original meanings was "to hand over" and that often means money or information that results in money. We're more inclined to call this an investment, and so it comes full circle. Tipping gets us better service next time, which makes it an investment, sometimes known as a bribe, rather than a reward. It's important to differentiate between a bribe and a reward, especially if you're raising children, and it's also important and can be the basic criteria for tipping.

If you believe that services may be required again in the future, it's wise to tip now because word gets around. If you never expect to have your hair rearranged, the trees trimmed, or your household belongings moved ever again in your lifetime, don't tip. If, however, you're building up your character for an everlasting future, I, for one, recommend that you hand over rewards often and generously.

You're Grabbing What?

Many people are worried about whether what they hear is the truth or "alternative" facts. It seems as though we not only don't trust each other to tell the truth, but we don't trust the English language to mean what it says. There are certain words we really don't like to use — such as liar, thief, crazy — and we probably should be careful of their use if we lack evidence. The problem is that one person's evidence may not be considered as valid as someone else's evidence.

There was a time that reporters couldn't print something without verifying it. Yet last week one of our television reporters said that "a gun bill had been introduced to permit guns in schools to keep people safe." She did not say that the sponsors claimed guns in the school would keep people safe, but stated it as a factual description of the bill. Did she lie? Of course not. But it's disturbing that she didn't know the difference between reporting it as a bill that would achieve certain results than as a bill that the sponsor claimed was designed to achieve a given result.

Speaking of language, the phrase that makes me want to tear the little bit of limp hair I have out of my skull is "gun grabbers." Think about it. What is probably meant is that the government is going to invade your home and person and confiscate your guns. How we, the government, are going to do this is unclear. Shall we grab the gun by the barrel? This might be possible if it's pointing at the gun holder's tummy, knee cap or foot, but pretty darn risky if it's pointed at us.

Perhaps we could grab it by the hammer. That would take a long reach, and I shudder to think of how it would sting if the trigger released the hammer. Maybe one could grab it by the trigger if one has really small fingers since someone else is already grasping the trigger. This is terribly up-close work, so I don't recommend it for those who weigh less than 140 pounds.

It's possible that the phrase led me to think of "grabbing" as solely a close-up activity, but that there could be some broad actions that didn't require personal risk. A law could be passed that prohibited grabbing a person's weapon. It would have to be specific. For example, if it's removed from a holster on the dresser, is it grabbing? Is it grabbing if it's snatched from a holster on someone's hip? If it's grabbed from someone's waist or, worse, his pocket, is that grabbing or does that fall into inappropriate contact?

Admittedly, if there are gun- free zones, then it follows that there will be grab-free zones, and that does seem like a good idea. After all, if guns don't kill people, it follows that guns also don't protect people. I think the argument is that only people kill people and so only people can keep other people safe … at least most of the time.

I wonder how my father and brother would have reacted to the idea that someone could or would grab their guns. Dad would probably have said, "Great, you can supply the meat for our family this winter." My brother would ask if you had any idea what the beaches at Normandy looked like when people decided to use guns to kill other people. The guns in our family, then and now, weren't viewed as weapons to kill people, but to bag food.

Perhaps before those who wish to carry concealed guns in schools and other public places should ask themselves some fundamental questions, like why they don't feel safe with other people or what kind of message we're giving children and young people about solving problems, or whether arming everyone protects or infringes on our liberty to voice opinions. Is it possible to hold open meetings or walk down a street with confidence when everyone is armed? It's one thing to have our thoughts challenged, it's another to have our person threatened.

Words mean something, and when we believe that restrictions on gun ownership and appropriate use means we're trying to confiscate people's property, we're spreading fear and encouraging us to arm ourselves against fellow citizens. Does that also mean that we can only keep ourselves safe from ideas by shooting them? Are our children, and all of us, only safe if we're willing to be violent?

Words speak the truth, and the truth will set us free. Grabbing guns may be catchy, but it doesn't accurately describe either truth or practical action.

CHAPTER 2

Blowing In the Wind

For some reason, the wind of the past few weeks became a metaphor for why our attempts to improve education are so frustrating. Trying to match efforts with results is a little like spitting in the wind and expect(orat)ing it to come back liquid gold. It won't happen unless we change directions, stop spitting and pay attention to the questions and recommendations teachers are voicing.

For years, I've advocated asking teachers how to change education so that more students grow into good citizens. If anyone knows, they do. Last week I learned about a group who held a summit and came up with some suggestions. This group of about 45 teachers (10 from Natrona County), who had received their National Board Certifications, summarized their recommendations in a report that one of its leaders, Mauro Diaz, said they intend to share, and continue to share, with boards, parents, legislators and community groups until action is taken.

Is there a more informed, experienced group to lead the way on educational change? The exciting thing about their report wasn't simply that they had some recommendations, but that they had the significant questions, questions that need to be discussed by all of us. These are the questions some people call "philosophical" and unnecessary. They seem to think like my grandmother, who called them "high-falluting" theoretical speculation. She didn't see them as foundational questions based on values and beliefs from which to build actions.

The teachers talked, as should we, about changing the qualifications and procedures for entering the profession ... the way we've organized schools, how children learn, and how teachers are provided continuing learning experience that results in higher student achievement. They also discussed educational leadership.

They didn't have the question I would add to the list, which is the purpose of education because they probably thought they knew that what they were doing, generally, was to prepare students for life in a democratic society.

Their first topics were how to prepare the teachers and how to stimulate student learning. Their main emphasis wasn't on curriculum or subject matter so much as the skills students need and how they could encourage student-driven opportunities to explore their world through reading, language, writing and math.

One of the problems of educational reform is that if one part of the system is changed, it affects all other parts. The summit teachers, however, started in a place that most school boards, legislators, state boards and other policy makers haven't started: with the preparation of teachers and the continuation of teacher learning.

It makes common sense that if one starts with the preparation and education of teachers, principals, etc., there will be changes in student learning, the organization and function of schools, and the scheduling and grouping of students. Instead, we seem to focus on student results without recognizing teaching as a fundamental part of the change process. Oh, we've blamed teachers, but we haven't questioned the programs that prepare them nor the system that places them.

More importantly, perhaps, is that we've instituted an accountability system that doesn't measure learning skills that are equally or more important than the information recalled. Indeed, most of us forget the information after awhile, but the skills we acquired are used and last a lifetime.

Do we really see the life skills of problem-solving, critical thinking, innovation and creativity as practical and even fundamental to success? If we do, and we say we do, it makes a difference how teachers are prepared, how students are taught and how learning is measured.

Maybe we need to de-emphasize the measuring of transitory factors in student learning, and start measuring the life skills that will serve the students in all the roles they'll assume in life. Skills can be measured — ask a musician, a carpenter, an artist, a mechanic, a teacher. And many teachers have embedded skills training into how they teach, but claim they could do more if they weren't diverted into teaching to a high-stakes measurement that "tests" a small part of what students need to learn.

Change is blowing in the wind, but we won't alter our directions until we listen, and it's hard to listen when we keep spitting out old solutions that come back in the same form we've sent them.

Budgets and Bulbs

There are two things that grab my attention this time of year: one is for pleasure and the other is a duty that I held for over 40 years and can't seem to get over.

The pleasure? Thinking of what to plant, knowing full well that the critters get to eat more than I do. But I love reading every catalogue, identifying space, inventorying pots and considering budget. Every year irises and daffodils and other wonderful things come up early and I'm out in the yard yelling, "get back, get back." I'm always amazed that these flowers poke through the snow without freezing, while other flowers take a lot of effort to get one bloom. The soil has to be fed, the water needs to be put on judiciously, and the deer have to be chased away.

I depend on my dog to intimidate the deer, but he barks at everything else that has the audacity to walk on our sidewalks or travel on our street, but he invites the deer into our yard by wagging his tail. The deer aren't solely to blame for disabling flowers since both the dog and the cat seem to think the flower beds are bathrooms or racing tracks. Still, I can hardly wait … for the planting season.

The other preoccupation that's ingrained as part of spring is budget-making. Since I worked for public agencies for 50 years, spring is budget-making time. I have definite ideas about public budgets, and recall with a smile the problems I had with a man named O'Brien in the Wyoming Department of Education.

He claimed all we needed to do was to increase every line item by 15 percent and we would have the funds we needed for the following year or two. I reminded him that he was the comptroller, not the budget-maker, and that the entire department needed to be involved in a process of setting goals, specifying activities and closely estimating what it was going to cost to accomplish our goals and provide services.

So, every year the entire staff would spend two days in retreat, figuring out what we wanted to do, why we wanted to do it, and what the cost would be. And every year, O'Brien would come to the retreat and just smile and shake his head.

I would go to the legislature knowing every single detail about the budget, and every year, they'd totally ignore the details and decide how many staff we ought to have, and why we shouldn't have travel money. In other words, year after year, for 12 years, O'Brien was right. I should have just added 15 percent.

But after planning approximately 24 education budgets during a lifetime in education, I still believe that public agencies should know where they're going and why, and that funds are the tools for getting there. Whether at the federal, state or local level, public education dollars should be spent nearest the students; agencies should remember that money belongs to the public; and there should be a direct relationship between budgets and goals.

It intrigues me when districts say that the money should be closest to the kids, but then keep a lot in the central office instead of distributing it to the schools. That's where the professional development funds should be, because school staff know what they need.

A couple of other notions I have, but no one asked about, are that the role of an administrative office should be to offer services rather than directions. Is it any wonder that agencies breathe a sigh of relief when I'm relieved of budgeting duties? I also believe that administrators should account for the use of funds.

I had a few good teachers back in the 1980s. It wasn't unusual to pick up the phone and hear Governor Ed Herschler growling, "Tell me why you're paying for a group to go into the wilderness area, Audrey." He paid attention just enough to keep everyone on their toes.

Since the wilderness trip was planned (under physical education), the group went. However, when the leader heard people coming through the brush and recognized the governor, he was sure he had come after him and he would be fired Monday morning. He wasn't, of course, but I never forgot that no matter how much responsibility the office held, there was always time to let people think that you checked everything.

I also learned there's a difference between being a comptroller, i.e., keeping track of the funds, and budget-making, i.e., determining how to use the fiscal tool reasonably. At least I tell myself that when I'm trying to figure out how to purchase $200 worth of bulbs and plants this spring.

I may have to cross tomato plants off the list. Last year they cost me $55.50 for each ripe tomato. I wonder if the animals that ate my tomatoes also ate my lettuce? It would make sense if they knew how to order bacon and if the squirrels transferred the tulip bulbs. There seems to be a relationship between bulbs and budgets after all.

Culture and Poverty

"Culture," we're told, is the art, customs, ideas and behavior of a group. After reading about the behavior of adult professionals at Natrona County High School last week, it seemed to me that it was the perfect time to talk about "culture."

Casper seems to have three major cultures: the culture of poverty, the culture of middle-class, and the "upper crust" culture. Oddly, both the middle-class cultures and the upper crust cultures seem to be adopting the characteristics associated with the culture of poverty.

Let's assume that there are characteristics of each of the three major categories. While the so-called middle-class culture has the characteristics of hope, hard work, spirituality, trust and community, for example, the culture of poverty is fatalistic, suspicious, depressed, untrusting and often lacking in moral values, or at least the ones promoted and exemplified by the middle-class, which is what most of us are.

The middle-class culture includes dozens of non-profits that try to provide helpful services to people in need. The problem is, agencies like Seton House, Joshua's Storehouse, Poverty Resistance, various church pantries and other public entities such as the Housing Authority, the Central Wyoming Rescue Mission, the Community Action Partnership, Goodwill and the Salvation Army can't solve the problems unless they assist individuals in moving out of the poverty culture into a culture of independence, optimism and hard work.

We seem to be drifting toward values such as self-interest, instant gratification, undisciplined freedom and just plain laziness. In this prosperous America, we don't seem to aspire to a culture that's enlightened, genteel, literate, polished or sophisticated. And that may be progress, for the Snobs don't rule anymore. On the other hand, substituting a culture of anti-intellectualism, instant gratification, violence and selfishness doesn't sound like a good idea, either.

I suppose we could live and let live more easily if we weren't convinced that a self-governing society can't maintain itself without a sense of loyalty, cooperation and optimism and a moral compass that includes a concern for the common good.

In contemporary America, the upper wealthy culture no longer represents the elegant, enlightened, genteel, literate, polished, sophisticated, highbrow, intellectual segment of the population that we all wish to emulate. We now seem to want the wealth, but are inclined to model and exhibit our most base characteristics in clothing, thinking and behavior.

Ruby Payne, who has done a considerable amount of research on poverty, for example, identifies some of the characteristics of the culture of poverty. "Poverty," she said, "is not simply economic." If it's situational, individuals make every effort to move out. If it's generational, it may also be emotional, mental, spiritual and/or physical poverty. With a little help, people move out of situational poverty, but generational poverty may consist of multiple "poverties" and becomes a way of life, or a culture.

There are two major institutions that are capable of lifting us out of the culture of poverty: one is the church and the other is the school. Both need to understand that providing food, understanding or sympathy don't necessarily help needy individuals or groups climb out of self-defeating cultures of poverty. Sometimes, charity encourages people to keep the circumstances they have.

Payne said there are four reasons people get out of the culture of poverty. They are education, key relationships, a special talent or skill and because it's too painful to stay in the group where they are.

I'm not sure that churches can be anything but charitable, but I'm convinced that schools need to be tougher. Schools need to create a culture of discipline, respect and hard work if children are to break the cycle of generational poverty. That means that the adults they deal with must be responsible adults, build caring relationships, have high expectations, provide moral and intellectual support, and empower students to make choices and take the consequences. Many teachers do, and most try, but they're operating within a system that encourages freedom without responsibility, rewards without effort, and actions without consequences.

Schools need rules, both written, and unwritten, that lift people out of a culture of poverty, and the most fundamental of all is the rule that for every action there is a consequence, i.e., if you don't attend regularly and do the work, you don't pass on to the next grade.

If culture is a way of living, we need to think about whether we're building a culture that encourages our darker selves or one that encourages and nurtures our better selves. Poverty defines more than our financial status; it's a picture of our spirit, our state of mind, our moral attitude and our respect for one another.

Ahhhh, Equality

It's no surprise that there's still gender bias in the world and even here in Wyoming in the state legislature, for example.

If one was born in the 1920s or '30s, it took us longer to recognize it than those born in the 1960s and later.

For example, I really didn't label it gender bias when one of my sons wished that I would be more like Rod's mom. She baked cookies, let the kids tear up the house and never said no to her only child.

Even though I baked 10 dozen peanut butter cookies a week in those days, somehow I didn't meet the criteria. If you messed the house, you helped clean the house, from two years old onward. If your friends wanted to wrestle or fist-fight, they were to go outside. If the music was too loud in the basement, go to the garage or Rod's house.

Maybe it was because I was a member, even chair, of the PTA and League of Women Voters, and the mental health association, and tried to get the city council and county commission to do things. Maybe they just wanted a mother who did more than iron 17 shirts every week, baked peanut butter cookies and insisted they make their beds.

I wondered what was so special about Rod's mother. And then I knew. She fulfilled the role of a mother completely. She never stepped out of it, and this mother did. I was out trying to change the world and that wasn't the role assigned to women, especially after the Big War. After all, we weren't in the decadent '20s anymore. Mom wasn't dancing and drinking, but she was talking a lot, trying to get people to do stuff.

Even though the first grandson, a 1970s kid, thought Gramma was different, he liked it because he got a lot of attention explaining that we sat in a fast-food parking lot during tornadoes in the Dakotas, but got to sleep and eat whenever we wanted, or he could brag that the "fuzz" stopped Gramma for speeding again, or because the highway patrol thought I had abducted a little kid who liked to stop at every bathroom from Wyoming to Minnesota. Somebody thought he was trying to escape, when he was simply fascinated with trying to make arches or hit targets.

If it was gender bias, and I believe it was, it took on a more serious tone in the work world. It was one thing when the men were introduced as "Dr." and I was introduced as "Mrs." or just plain Audrey. After all, I was supposed to be modest ... mother and grandmother insisted upon it when they recognized that they had a show-off in the family.

But it wasn't acceptable after 12 years in state government when some legislators publicly said I was ruthless. They decided this after believing information given to them by an agency informant who spent all his time looking through partisan glasses and not doing a lick of work. I suppose "ruthless" could be applied to someone who thought that if you collected a paycheck from public funds, you should perform a public service.

While I was in the Wyoming Department of Education, another Casperite joined state government. His name was Ken Erickson and he had quite a bit to say about some of the state employees and whether they were working hard enough. His comments were applauded, but when I said these things in a much milder manner, I had no "credibility." It was odd, because both Ken and I were among the few people telling the truth.

I had no knowledge of how Cindy Hill ran the agency, but I was sympathetic to any woman who was the butt of the kind of cruelty and sexism demonstrated by the legislators who wiped out her position until the court said they couldn't do it. They tried to wipe out the only appointed position the state superintendent had in the 1980s ... the deputy state superintendent, chosen by the elected superintendent.

Yes, Virginia, there is gender bias. If you wish to prove it, ask what action was taken about two male superintendents prior to Hill, who were demonstrably incompetent.

But I'm not mad, I just reached the age where I could be plenty ornery without penalty. After all, I don't have to get a job, I know that power is delusional, and I don't have to be loved to love.

Elder-Hostile or Save Our Students?

After the past few weeks, I was tempted to form an "Elder-Hostile" group. You know the kind of week where you blame everything on being ignored or considered senile? The kind of week where, stressed in your sleep, you can't tell when you awake whether your nightmare was real or not?

It's a good thing Sunday came and the minister gave a sermon about joy. What happened to my joy, I asked myself? We really don't need more hostility, but isn't there some joy in righteous indignation if it accomplishes something?

Why is everybody angry? Kids have never been more pampered (or neglected), but they're angry. Older students bully each other because they're angry; adults believe that they're entitled and when they get what they need, they're still angry because they need more ... of something.

It seems that people are impoverished even though some are rich, are employed but hate their jobs, and complain that their government is enslaving them even when they have more freedom than practically any people on earth. We want more services, more protection and more recreation, but are mad about our country's debt.

Would I find joy by quitting everything I'm doing? Of course not. But I must do the things in which I find joy, and so must you. I found no joy, but lots of anger being a school board trustee.

There was no joy in trying to give ideas people didn't want ... not for me, not for the group. Students hadn't learned more, and teachers hadn't been allowed the freedom they needed to teach what really counted. Teachers struggled to teach what they knew was needed, but recall of information took precedence over creativity, imagination, critical thinking and friendships. I had not improved results, nor had the group. Some seeds were planted, and will bear fruit, but not fast enough for me, or the kids.

Truth is, we find joy in struggle which gets results. We know what made the spirits soar: accomplishments like the great Reagan concert. When you fill up with what humans can do with their voices, their artistic ability, with any one of the talents that enoble the individual, you know very well which actions don't. These talents distinguish us from the other creatures inhabiting this planet.

Resigning with a year left to serve on the board wasn't easy. I apologize, but I couldn't match my experience and abilities with what the board thought they wanted or needed. It doesn't make sense when we keep doing what doesn't work, but I attended a Methodist college that reminded us every day that we had been blessed and must keep giving because we OWED our community. They never told us what to do when whatever we had to offer wasn't needed or wanted. Considered particularly obnoxious was one of my lifelong, primary objects of joy: provoking discussions that led to better answers. Some people value harmony more than candid discussion, forgetting that harmony consists of several parts.

Trying to give what isn't wanted is like giving a hockey player a ping-pong paddle. The gift needs to match up with the style and purpose of the potential recipient.

I need time to support and experience more music, drama and art. I need to teach more and learn more. That's where the joy lies, along with reading and writing, visiting more friends, talking to grown sons and daughters, encouraging grandchildren and holding great-grandchildren. These things are nutrition for the soul.

Besides, on Monday morning at 5 a.m., I got a "sign." My Amish clock that had been idle for two years tolled, but not five chimes; it tolled just once. When it tolled again, twice at 6 a.m., but pointed at 2 a.m., I asked for whom the bell tolls, and decided on the spot it was for me, unless I sought joy.

I want to use my energy to change the important things that need changing such as the quality and quantity of education many students are getting. I'll search, need be, until I find others with similar goals who will have the talents I don't possess.

Running the Red

If you were to guess where people are most careful about obeying traffic laws, would it be in school zones? If you said yes, you'd be wrong. Syd Webb, head of transportation for the Natrona County School District, told me that his school bus drivers report daily that people not only speed through school zones, but pass buses with flashing yellow and red lights, and flashing stop signs.

Why, I said to myself, would people not obey the law to drive 20 mph through school zones or, worse, drive around big yellow buses with flashing warning signs? To find out, I visited with four school bus drivers and the examples told by Leah, Debbie, Lonnie and Steve were perplexing, outrageous and bizarre to say the least, and far exceeded the excuses for speeding through school zones.

We all understand that people are late for work, talking on their cell phones, worried about whether they're going to run out of gas, still sleepy, thinking about what to make for dinner, and don't realize that they're in a school zone, or don't realize they're going 30 mph or more.

I recall the story about the State Superintendent of Instruction, Velma Linford, being ticketed for speeding in a school zone. Instead of saying she was sorry and that she was thinking of how to improve services to all the schools in Wyoming, she said she didn't do it. No doubt she claimed, as did some of the state employees during the 55 mph limit in the Herschler years, that she had only been going 23 in a 20 mile zone. One state employee told me that he had not been doing more than 75 in a 55 mph limit and it was unfair to limit his use of a state car, so that excuse has been around for awhile.

But deliberately going around buses with flashing lights defies all explanations. Often, the drivers are parents who have just dropped off or picked up their children. Why they don't know their behavior endangers other children is the mystery of the century, whether they're in a loading zone in front of a school or on the highway. The yellow or red lights are signalling "CAUTION." The red signals "STOP."

It has gotten so bad in rural areas that some bus drivers pick up children on only the right side of the road and turn around to pick up those on the left. So if you're wondering why those closest to town on the left hand side of the highway are the last to be picked up, blame the person who passes a bus with four flashing yellow or red lights (and a flashing stop sign) at 65 mph.

The drivers told me that those who go around a bus with yellow or red lights don't want to wait, and don't understand that drivers pause for several reasons, but the main one is that every child who boards or exits a bus must be checked off on a roll sheet. Why? Because drivers are responsible for noting who gets on and who gets off. School districts aren't in the habit of losing kids.

Yet when parents go around stopped or about-to-stop school buses, they jeopardize someone's child who's getting on or off. That's why drivers have trained children not to walk behind the bus, and to stop immediately if the driver honks. Drivers watch the rear view mirror once those yellow lights go on for drive-around cars because once the red lights go on, the bus door opens and children expect to enter or exit safely.

It doesn't make sense to risk hitting a child, but believe it — drivers ignore the law on the average of 10 times in the morning and 10 times in the afternoon. In a recent survey of community attitudes about a potential bond issue, the majority of adults approved of spending on safety issues, yet there are adults ignoring the safety of students.

Don't you wonder what makes people act as they do? What possible explanations could be given? Here are some of them: I didn't see the bus; I was on my cell and diverted; I didn't know you were supposed to stop; I didn't know the amber lights meant the bus was going to stop; I thought I could get around before the kids got off; I thought the bus driver would see me going around and keep the kids on the bus; I didn't do it; There weren't any police there; What are you going to do about it (with finger gesture)?

Neither the police nor the bus drivers can solve the problem by themselves. It's a community problem that may be reduced if there's a penalty every time. Perhaps new technology could be installed on buses to verify the license number, the identity of the car and the identity of the driver. All are required in order to fine the driver about $750, and unless a policeman is on scene, the bus driver's word is pitted against the violator's in court.

One school bus driver actually left the stopped bus to tell a driver trying to go around that it was illegal to do so and she could be fined if she did it. The bus driver was reported to her boss for "threatening" the violator.

There's one other explanation, but I don't want to believe it: this is a free country and we can do what we want. I don't believe running the red is a matter of individual freedom, when the results are potentially so serious, do you? But then, I was taught that freedom is so precious, the price is responsibility.

You Know You're In Wyoming When ...

When my husband announced that he had been transferred from St. Paul, Minn., to Casper, Wyo., he assured me that Casper had a League of Women Voters. Since the League had always provided a quick and thorough introduction to a new community, I was convinced ... even though I wasn't sure about the location of a place called Casper.

The LWV welcome was immediate. We were invited to a ranch barbecue where I was placed on a horse that instinctively knew that I had never ridden and reacted accordingly. But we had a great time and found the west to have warm, open people as well as vast land with very few trees.

It wasn't long before I met Nancy and Brooks Nichols and although we were of different political parties, we became friends; in fact, differing but common interests in "political" issues seemed to invite instant intimacy. We were stimulated by the spirited discussion.

Invited to a party by the Nichols one evening, Nancy was enthusiastically describing her attendance at a state banquet. She said, "I just couldn't believe that I was sitting next to Kenny Sailors ... he was a star UW basketball player, you know ... and I said to Stan, 'Isn't this the most exciting event?'"

"Is Stan your son?" I asked.

"Oh no," she said. "Stan is the governor ... Stan Hathaway."

That became the watershed moment when I understood the difference between Minnesota and Wyoming. Only in Wyoming could you sit with the governor on your left and be more thrilled with the athlete on your right.

It should have prepared me for working with state officials, but I'm still in awe of the down-to-earth modesty that was displayed for many years in Wyoming politics. It wasn't unusual in the 1980s to pick up the phone in the Wyoming Department of Education and hear the governor growl, "Audrey, what's this expenditure for a wilderness trip?"

Ed Herschler reviewed just enough of the thousands of invoices to keep everyone alert and careful. He said he didn't think having a half-dozen people wandering around the wilderness at taxpayer expense was wise.

Governing was close and personal in those days. It seemed like everyone not only knew "Ed," but that Ed knew everyone by name. Though a little more formal, that was true about Win Hickey, Cliff Hansen, Stan Hathaway, Dave Freudenthal and Mike Sullivan. It was also true about Gale McGee, Malcolm Wallop, Al Simpson and William Harrison. Regardless of party affiliation, one could write for help and receive it, or a lengthy explanation of why not. But then politics began to change.

Or maybe it's the world that's changed, and some of us, like every "older" person, long for the way things used to be. There just seems to be a vast difference between people like Tom Stroock, Dan Sullivan, Diemer True, Pat Meenan, Bill Curry, Warren Morton, John Wold and some of the single-issue individuals now in government. Maybe it has to do with a sense of service and a search for the common good. Maybe the already successful people who ran for office didn't need the title, but felt they could contribute. Maybe it was because there was a respect for getting the questions straight before the answers were examined and chosen.

Whatever the difference, it's disturbing. We've entered a period when we don't seem to respect those we've chosen to represent us. We disdain our own government rather than honor it as the way we individually decide how to live together.

If the former Wyoming leaders seem to be giants, it's because we now seem to choose party over character, promises over evidence, and ignorance over research. They didn't need adulation, but they demanded respect for themselves and the institutions that everyone built together for the past 200 years.

Maybe our folks and our culture taught our generation to serve because they believed that to whom much was given, much was expected. Maybe we forgot what Mike Sullivan said about Wyoming being a small town with long streets.

Litter Did I Know

It took over 80 years, but this week I finally understand why it's called cat "litter." My book club met on a stormy Tuesday when it snowed, sleeted and then snowed again. I shoveled walks 10 minutes before my guests arrived, and then discovered that the porch had iced over. Not knowing whether table salt would do the trick, I grabbed the cat litter and littered it.

Two days later, I'm still vacuuming cat litter. It's literally scattered over every room in the house.

It couldn't happen at a more auspicious time, since my office is also littered with files. Yes, I'm downsizing again ... this time by cleaning files. Did I say cleaning? I'm going through every single folder in every single file and throwing out practically nothing.

My whole life is just a litter before me. Thank goodness it consists of evidence of public involvement, so I can deliver it to the archives at Casper College and elsewhere. But first, I have to part with it because without these files I may have no memory at all. For several stormy days I've discovered things I've forgotten and am now moving those memories from one file to another.

Since I'm trying to write my memoirs without a good memory, it is hard to throw out documents. For example, I discovered really bad poetry that I wrote in junior high. Should I save it for my grandchildren and say something amusing about it, use it as a lesson of sorts, or throw it out? It isn't as though I could contrast it with my recent poetry since I gave up trying to rhyme after taking a poetry class in college and realizing that I would never write poetry ... ever.

What, pray tell, should I do with all the letters my children's father wrote to me? Shall I show what a foolish 20-year-old he was when I'm unwilling and unable to produce my own letters? I haven't read them for 60 years, and so by all the rules of usage, I should burn them. But I have the heart of a historian, the mind of a philosopher and very curious off-spring.

Two of the days I spent reviewing files were spent on the League of Women Voters. I joined the League in the 1950s and remember being attacked during the McCarthy days. We had sponsored the Freedom Agenda pamphlets about government, and a McCarthy-ite named Fulton Lewis Jr. accused the League of being sympathetic to communism. My mother-in-law called in a panic and said, "Get out of the League!"

Instead, I volunteered to read every single pamphlet and highlight anything that looked like a Democrat, let alone a Communist, might have written, since almost everyone in our unit was a Republican at the time. I pointed out a few liberal-sounding sentences, and we all stayed in the League.

As I read the remarkable positions taken by the League of Women Voters in the 1950s and '60s here in Casper, the study that went into issues before a position was taken, and the laudatory letters from mayors, legislators and Congressmen, I couldn't help but be nostalgic.

I'm convinced that we need a non-partisan group more than ever. Some reliable group needs to bring back the habit of considering all solutions and consequences before taking a stand and informing the public. It certainly would cut down on the litter. Another thing that occurred to me was that the League gave women power because there was a definite relationship between being informed and influencing policy.

The League of Women Voters actually believed and practiced the idea that democracy required an informed citizenry. When did the two major parties begin promoting the idea that party membership relieved people of the responsibility to inform themselves before voting? If voters really believe that all they need to know is which party is behind a candidate's name, maybe it's time for the parties to interview and approve of those who carry the party name. After all, platforms and philosophy should be the hallmark of the candidates' party affiliations.

Individuals shouldn't be able to run under a party label when they're supported by a group that doesn't subscribe to that party. For example, is a person associated with the Tea or Liberty "party" actually a Republican? And is an individual who subscribes to the Libertarian or Progressive "party" actually a Democrat? An individual without affiliation should be able to file and run, but they shouldn't be able to hide behind a party label if they really don't endorse a party's philosophy and plan of action.

It's amazing what thoughts occur when vacuuming cat litter or trying to distribute old files. We could use some objectivity to disperse litter, personally and politically.

Losing Wyoming

Just about the time one thinks there couldn't be more disrespect for professional educators, the legislature offers one more insult. They're now going to offer a bill to create a panel of parents and teachers to consider getting rid of the standards for language and arts!?

Such an action is not only insulting, it embarrasses the state of Wyoming. It signals that we're not part of the UNITED states of America, but that we're so out of touch, we don't understand that a) high standards are needed nationwide, and b) scores of teachers and parents, state superintendents and governors were involved in creating the standards for students wherever they live.

Finally, and perhaps most importantly, it appears that legislators have no idea about what it means to educate children from families who may have lived in poverty for two or more generations. This is a different culture, and if we don't recognize this and understand what it means to the classroom teacher, it will be impossible to lift the students from the culture that they've inherited.

There's not a single other profession that's treated so shabbily by a group of amateurs who think they know more than those who are educated to teach and have the experience and knowledge to try to solve the problem, most of which can be laid to the results of poverty.

Perhaps that's because poverty is viewed solely as being without the necessities of food, health care and housing. But it's more than that, and it's about time we look at the characteristics and stop trying to give it a political "fix" rather than consider it a cultural problem that must be addressed.

Right here in Natrona County, 38 percent of the school children (and it's more if you consider their preschool brothers and sisters) are receiving free and reduced lunches, and over 300 backpacks full of food are sent home with hungry children every Friday. The packs contain six meals and snacks and are probably shared with siblings.

But this is the tip of the iceberg and token of what the schools are trying to do for these children. If one considers the characteristics rather than the symptoms of poverty, then what the educators are doing deserves a commendation by the general public, parents and legislators, rather than a bow to the far right that has some notion that it's more important to view all nationwide efforts for children as some ploy to take away their individual liberties.

Why would we add one more action by Wyoming officials that makes us look like backwoods ninnies before the country and the world? When are the thinking people of this state going to insist on a return to rationality?

What, specifically, in the standards do we wish to wipe out? And when shall we question the tendency in Wyoming to view every other profession (doctors, lawyers, engineers, etc.) as knowing what they're doing, but thinking the average citizen knows more about how a variety of children learn and how to teach them?

Ask any retired or working teacher what the morale is like here in Casper when teachers and schools are doing dozens of things that a parent ought to be doing, without respect and support from the community. They will tell you, morale hasn't been any lower in their memory. And why? Because they not only aren't praised, they're disrespected. It takes total dedication to continue doing a job with so few social, psychological and symbolic rewards.

Storm Musings

I'm inclined to get introspective when the snow falls. This may result from growing up in International Falls, Minn., where we rarely spoke to anyone until spring.

When the city did such a great job of helping people clean up, and when neighbors helped each other, and everybody from the power company to the garbage collectors were efficient and effective, I became philosophical, especially in light of how our government in D.C. is behaving.

At least government in Casper really works! We should all congratulate the city and every part of it for responding the way they did after our heavy, destructive snowfall. I think we'd all like to believe that the reason we need government is to collectively do what one person can't do alone, and that "we" are the government and if it isn't going right, we're the ones who have to correct it at the ballot box.

Since I convinced myself that America's grand experience has survived self-interest, bigotry, the Salem Witch Trials and McCarthyism, and it's evident that Casper government is functioning very well, I could turn my attention to lighter activities such as baking and cleaning out the kitchen drawers and perhaps even get some profound lessons from these activities.

So, between cutting fallen limbs with a hack saw (little, but sharp) and trying to rake piles of leaves in the snow, I began an inside retrospect. Once having sharpened the mind with healthy activities, I counted on ignoring complaints from the body.

It was the right choice. I had no idea that cleaning out drawers is almost as exciting as discovering potential presents I put in the Christmas closet a year ago.

What a thrill to find a mango slicer and a cherry pitter and other unique items that we need when we need them. It's a surprise to find an apple corer, garlic and lemon squeezers, melon baller and tea strainer.

There's a profound philosophical issue involved, too, not unlike the political dilemma encountered by a yard full of tree limbs. If things aren't being used or have been made useless, do we commit an acquisitive, unethical act by throwing them out, making them usable, or by expecting someone else to do something about it? Is there a role for government to provide occasional services whether they're needed by everybody all the time or not? Shall we discard tools (assistance) that someone can use, even though we don't need them or want them?

Is finding a recipient of a garlic or lemon squeezer, however, our responsibility and is this the same question as finding or providing services for the poor or the incapable (or even the lazy)? Does anyone under 50 even use an outdated cherry pitter? Perhaps someone could use them so that we didn't have to take the responsibility of overspending. Similarly, should the "feds" shut down the parks, children's food programs, Social Security payments or health insurance just because they don't need them?

Somewhere there has to be a life lesson that makes sense. Maybe fruit makes as much sense ("Life is just a bowl of cherries" or "If you get a lemon, make lemonade") as those "nuts" in Washington.

Maybe we should solemnly swear that we're the government and together we can find the right use for it. As for the utensils, the responsible thing to do is match the food to the tool, just as we match the government to what the majority of its citizen said they wanted when they voted.

The city of Casper — citizens, government, churches and agencies — could offer itself as a model. I find heavy snow taxing on both the leaves and the mind, don't you?

Move Over?

Last week I read an article in the Casper Star-Tribune that indicated that people were moving toward the middle politically. I thought that sounded like a good idea. Maybe we should all move to become "centrists" and stop being so extreme.

But then I wondered whether this was really the problem. Maybe it's all right to have extreme ideas. Maybe, however, we should stop having the answers before we know the question. Maybe it's the predictability of our answers that's the problem.

Is it significant that only the Bible tells us to be moderate in all things? Or are those who tell us that moderation is for the weak and that extremism is no vice correct? Do the meek really inherit the earth? I wonder who wants to.

Personally, I think moderation isn't the answer, at least consistently. I think we need more mobility in moving back and forth between the "either" and the "or." This permits us to hold conflicting values at the same time, which we seem to find natural. Even more importantly, it gives us a chance to actually move toward rational solutions. How do we compromise unless we begin with a definite, extreme point of view?

A few years back someone wrote a book called "Who Moved My Cheese?" I didn't agree with the thesis of the book, which is when someone moves your cheese, you need to go find it. Instead, I believe we move our own cheese. It's the height of timidity to adjust to someone else's actions. On the other hand, it's too bullish to try to move everyone else's cheese.

Maybe the answer is to stand firm enough to elicit, even demand, a conversation that moves everybody to a new place. Compromise, I told myself, isn't the state of indifference, but a way of thinking about other possibilities. If we don't have a position (cheese), how are we to compromise?

And if someone moves my cheese, I think I'll resist. I want to move my own cheese, but in order to do that, I have to consider options, not just supply the same old solutions for getting more cheese or moving the supply I already have.

I learned from the Book of Common Prayer that we have to "keep the mean between extremes and that there's too much stuffiness in refusing to keep the mean, and too much easiness in admitting a variation from it."

Doesn't the same thing apply to politics and everyday life? There was a little boy who always put the knickknacks back where they had been after his mother moved them. Admittedly, some resistance to change is expected if safety and security is to be maintained. But anyone with a tendency to keep everything where it is certainly limits the freedom for the individual and those around him. I should know ... I married him.

Whether it's a knickknack or cheese metaphor, it's a lot healthier to move our thoughts to a different place than to keep them where they've always been.

I suppose being extreme can be healthy, providing we don't use our old thoughts to keep us where we've always been. It's good news if Americans are beginning to move toward the middle, but we need to redefine compromise. It's important to hang on to our cheese, especially if it represents our values. It seems to me that there are various ways to implement our values or eat our cheese if we remember that we're still in charge of our cheese.

So move your thoughts and actions where, when and how you want. Just don't let anyone else move them and then expect you to adjust.

Save the Honors

I noticed that Casper was designated the "best" on two things last week: most friendly to motorists and most hazardous for bikers and pedestrians; Wyoming was designated the least "transparent" government.

Like you, I said to myself, it's not always great to be #1, and I couldn't help but wonder what other honors we might not want for Casper or ourselves.

Do we really appreciate being in a town friendly to those who speed, go through stop lights and around school buses and pull up so far in the pedestrian crosswalk we can't see what's coming from the left when we want to turn right? Frankly, I would rather the police gave more tickets than the average number of tickets. Better a ticket trap than a pedestrian purgatory or biker's hell.

Wyoming won the title for non-transparency in government. Being the least open isn't an honor we hoped to achieve, even in a state where privacy, mind-your-own-business and "rugged" individualism are sacred. We meant people, not government.

The truth is, we don't want our communities or our individuals to stand out, either big winners or big losers. We really want everyone to be in the middle someplace, if the middle is a bit right of the political spectrum. We don't like contention, but we suspect unanimous, especially in elected agencies.

We don't admire ignorant or illiterate, but we also are mighty uncomfortable with brilliant and literate. The latter should live back east somewhere, and the former down south somewhere.

When we say we don't like extremes, we mean outside the "normal" in Casper or Wyoming. The fact that some of us see the "normal" every now and then as extreme probably means that we're not normal. One Lake Wobegon is not like another Lake Wobegon, where everyone is average.

So, I say, save your honors. Tell those who collect statistics to give first place or last place to others. Once we think about it, the list of "honors" we don't want is really long.

We want sunshine, but not too much, and wind, but not too much, and rain or snow when we order it. We want workers who will take directions, but save us from those individualists who want to decide when to come to work, what the duties are, and how long they want to stay.

Last week in the park, two little girls pointed me out as "the bag lady" and I resent that. I may be old and I may be baggy, but who uses the word lady anymore? We're women, and we're only ladylike when trying not to have extreme opinions.

As for our city, we don't want to be a city with the most weapons, the most autos, the most bounced checks, the most drug arrests, the most suicides, the most drinking, the most poverty, the least parenting, the lowest test scores.

It's nice to be a city with more than an average amount of statues and other art, museums, musicians, performances and health facilities. We just don't want to have more than anybody, or less than everybody.

We can be proud without being vain, and modest without being ashamed. As Peggy Curry used to say, "We can be tough but tender."

Save the "best" and "least" honors for some other city or some other people … unless, of course, it's for best debaters, scientists, artists, choirs, actors, athletes. We might like our children honored if they're not just average!

Speak Up

A few weeks ago I was given a white paper prepared by teachers who had received their national certificates and decided to meet to discuss findings and proposals in four areas: school organization, entry into the teaching profession, student learning and leadership and advocacy.

Many people I meet have talked about grouping students, and so I shall begin with that issue. Among the group's proposals was that students should be grouped by ability rather than age.

I rather like that idea, but there are a couple of obstacles to consider. The group could progress at their pace, but the teacher would still be challenged by individuals who needed a faster pace or with students who needed a slower pace in some subjects, since it's possible to be a genius in math and not so good in history. And what happens to the student who may be of academically higher ability, but whose emotional or social maturity isn't at the same level?

It wasn't unusual in early America to have a six-year-old in the same class with a 17-year-old. When is an age difference irrelevant, and when isn't it? I attended a small country school in the 2nd grade and learned at a faster pace because we were allowed to listen to what the others, including the 8th graders, were doing. The teacher never discouraged curiosity by saying, "Pay attention to your own work" or "Mind your own business," and so we had an accelerated experience. She did say, "Sit up straight and put your buttocks against the back of the seat" and I never figured out what that had to do with learning, but I learned in a hurry that it had something to do with respecting the teacher or you'd get in trouble at home.

A lot of people believe, however, that it's wrong to separate the robins from the blue jays, and their point is that it isn't democratic. Others contend that there's bound to be a lowering of standards when children with very low abilities and interests are combined with those of high or enriched abilities. Personally, I think there should be high standards and a broad scale that recognizes the difference between learners, and then uses both objective and subjective ways of assessing

— with the parent — where the student is on that scale.

Another reader, a local businessman, suggested that if students progress faster than others, they graduate in less than 12 years. This idea would probably work only if each student had an individual education plan (IEP), and in some contemporary classes they do. However, too often the teacher isn't given any credit for recognizing different learning styles or time-lines by officials who make policy and install standardized tests.

One question about the system leads to yet another, and if action is taken before the whole picture is clear, it's like playing dominoes: substitute one piece and they all fall. It's like building the roof before the foundation is laid.

Some of us would like further questions and discussion about the length of the school day, and why we're still scheduling in respect of an agrarian society. What would be the advantages of having school year-round with two weeks off every 18 weeks? Why must it take everybody 13 years to get a high school diploma?

What kind of skills should students have when they finish public schools? The Summit Group asks what would happen if 20 percent of students' time was given to them to pursue their own passions. If goals were set and accountability were part of the process, why not?

Would we re-think how we know if a student is learning if we took the number of hours used for testing and compared it, dollar-for-dollar, with the rise of one digit in test scores? If we could measure the relationship between funds and learning, would it give us the answer to how to improve? Would more or less money produce better results? What evidence do we have to claim there's a positive or negative correlation?

Finally, I wonder what would happen if all parents had to sign a contract that makes them full partners in the teaching and learning transaction. When did we stop believing that educating a child was a joint operation among students, parents and community, and begin blaming teachers for a major cultural shift that's affecting students?

When teachers speak, we should listen.

Too Much Charity?

Is it possible to be too charitable in spite of the admonishment in Corinthians that "charity is greater than hope and faith"? It has always seemed to me that service was more important than charity, probably because I've always had more time than money. In my opinion, if charity is really greater than faith and hope, it's because the biblical definition includes giving of self as well as wealth.

It's always heartening to realize how many people in Casper and Wyoming give thousands of unpaid hours, worth millions of dollars, to community programs and projects, and I applaud their service.

Yet I wonder whether more than 45 agencies in Casper receiving and distributing food adds up to duplication of efforts, is too much charity, or lends itself to duplicity by receivers. It doesn't seem to be the most efficient and effective way to tackle the issue of hungry people or the broader issue of poverty. There's little doubt about the charitable intentions ... almost all of the food banks are staffed by volunteers. A few actually have created paying jobs for people, but whether volunteer or paid, magnanimous or self-interested, they've distributed tons of free food. I just hope that these short-term solutions to hunger don't have some long-term unintended consequences like building a dependent rather than self-sufficient society, or helping us ignore the causes and consequences of poverty.

Some of the short-term results are these: there is more competition among the agencies for food, while duplication becomes more widespread, and the number of families that go from pantry to pantry produces either waste of food, the sale of food or a shortage of food for others.

Isn't it possible to build more communication and coordination among those trying to help, and at the same time consider and do something about the causes as well as the results of poverty?

If we could improve the process of feeding the hungry, maybe we could use our time and funds more judiciously. There's no question that as caring and generous people, we must feed the poor. More than half the people in poverty and in need of food are children. Who wants children to be hungry? School districts have expanded feeding to breakfast as well as lunch, and churches, especially, can provide over the weekend. Yet the number of programs multiply because people are decent, generous and charitable.

Would it be more efficient if there was a central agency that collects all the food and then distributes it? If there were a central agency, maybe the sub-stations should all have the same criteria that qualify people for the amount of food they need. If records were shared, would it eliminate duplication by agencies and the ability of some individuals to pick up more than they need? Perhaps there should be four major banks or collection points north, south, east and west of town that, in turn, deliver to agencies in that part of town.

Solutions aren't easy to come by, but if the community is to provide help to all the residents who need it, shouldn't every agency collecting and disseminating food have basic qualifications to determine individualized family needs and have a system of keeping records with information available to all agencies? Shouldn't every agency collecting food or funds be accountable to the pubic that contributes either time, food or funds? Without some coordination and cooperation among providers, the whole process is not only duplicative but open to corruption.

Most people want to help those in need, but they don't want to be ripped off by the few who take advantage. Without some coordination and cooperation among providers, giving food is a short-term solution. More than anything, the charitable public wants their help to count in making a stronger, better community.

Suffragette Mary Wollstonecraft had it right when she said, "It is justice, not charity, that is wanting in this world." Maybe we need to be aware of another biblical admonishment ... that charity can cover up a multitude of sins.

People In Our Circumstances

When I was young, in the 1930s and '40s, one of the most frustrating and irritating rules my parents would insist upon was "people in our circumstances don't ..." I'm not sure I knew whether they were talking about our financial situation due to the Depression, which was temporary, or about a belief system that destiny had dictated and was, therefore, permanent.

Were they caught up in an ideology or belief system, or were they saying that the circumstances had dictated both our ideas and our actions? Perhaps I'll never know whether they intended to discourage or motivate me.

But I thought about it again last week when someone quoted scripture extensively to justify what seemed to me to be discriminating against a whole class of people. I wondered when an idea becomes a system of viewing life rather than a thought that may or may not produce successful action.

Do we follow a system of ideas and principles in an inflexible way in order to have some certainty in our lives? And does certainty pretty well rule out things like spontaneity, joy, creativity and adventure? Do circumstances dictate our actions, or do our actions dictate circumstances?

If we believe that we're the victims of circumstance, do we develop a way of thinking, viewing and acting? I wondered about that again when I visited Joshua's Storehouse last week. If circumstances left the individuals and families without food, did they believe that the conditions would change or that they could change them? Or did some of them accept the notion that they couldn't provide for themselves and that others had a responsibility to do so? I wondered if they had lost hope.

It's not ideas that are our downfall; it's when we develop a system that's the answer to every problem or challenge, regardless of what the question is. For example, if we believe that taxes are bad, we can't concede that without them we wouldn't have services such as water, garbage collection, streets, etc. If we believe "government" is bad, we can't contemplate what anarchy is like.

It's ironic that we seem to have rigid ideologies about some things, but make adjustments to the only principles we've been commanded to follow. They don't really say, "Thou shall not kill ... unless you don't like someone" or "Thou shall not steal ... unless you have the opportunity." The Ten Commandments constitute a total system or ideology that's not conditional, yet we adjust this system but adopt social and political ideologies that are much more harmful to us.

It still seems to me that carrying a rigid system of standards that's applied to everything does limit our possibilities. On the other hand, adhering to 10 universal principles would make all our lives richer.

It's when one system of beliefs is applied to all issues that we go astray because that system provides automatic answers that don't recognize any ambiguity at all. "Doubt is never a pleasant condition, but certainty is an absurd one" (Voltaire).

We all seem to have at least one belief system that's inviolate, but as human beings, aren't we expected to hold on to opposite ideas at the same time? After all, humans are the only creatures we know who can do that. Maybe that's because our brain has two hemispheres.

Isn't ambiguity what makes us capable of being persuaded? Isn't it the absence of certainty that gives the other person the benefit of the doubt? What do we mean that circumstances prevent us from action? Circumstances change, and today's system is yesterday's collection of dumb ideas.

It seems to me that if I were parenting today, I'd never tell my offspring that "people in our circumstances don't ..." I'd tell them that it's their obligation to change the circumstances because my ideas on citizenship are quite definite, maybe even rigid.

Whaaat?

I recently took the dog in for his annual bath and grooming, and when I picked him up, I not only was scolded, but the price was increased 42 percent. I didn't mind the cost, but resented the implication that I didn't pamper this dog that sits on my lap when he's too big to be a lap dog. But what really struck me as odd is, why I would come to a dog groomer if I was able to bathe and groom my dog myself?

The incident, however, made me think about other things people say that sound like they really don't understand why you've come to them for services. For example, though well-intentioned, why do doctors ask you how you're feeling? If you felt great, you wouldn't be in their office.

Why does a person who agrees to clean your house complain if it's dirty? Or worse, why did my mother clean before the cleaning person came? Did she think the cleaning person would tell everyone in town that her house wasn't clean unless she cleaned it first?

It's always embarrassing to overdraw one's personal bank account, especially if you're in charge of a multi-million dollar agency budget, but is it logical for the teller to explain that you're overdrawn because you wrote too many checks? I suppose that's a better explanation than concluding you can't add, subtract or do other simple arithmetic. The teller should have suggested that I get an overdraft account.

Personally, I have to admit that I was almost 40 years old before I knew income was credit and outgo was a debit, I think. Way back in 1970, I took the job as Executive Director for United Way of Natrona County. They didn't know that I would have to bring home an adding machine that weighed 20 pounds and was larger than my toaster, and a double entry book that was as big as the coffee table, because I wasn't an accountant. The point is, I had a lot to learn in a hurry and so I called my father-in-law, an executive with Ford Motor Company, who explained that in an agency where people made pledges, there were debits and that they were reduced by credits (or was it vice versa?) and that if I couldn't keep track, to always remember the debits were toward the window.

I'm still not too clever about my money, and that made me doubly cautious about public money.

Beauticians, or hairstylists, or whatever master stylists call themselves, ask you how you want your hair cut, curled or fashioned. If you knew, wouldn't you just do it at home?

I believe most of these people are trying to be helpful or are trying to demonstrate how democratic they are, when they really intend to do what they can do with what they've got, so why do they ask?

My favorite helpful hint is, "Don't put the plastic bag over your head." Well, I suppose not, but when it's raining or snowing, it might be all right to place it over your head. Shouldn't they just tell us not to put it over the nose or mouth if we want to breathe? I suppose that if they could talk to you, they'd say, "Did you find yourself short of breath when you put the bag over your head?"

A friend of mine got a new iron, and the instructions warned her not to iron her clothes while she was wearing them. Why do real people write these kinds of instructions?

I don't think one could do this anyway, unless they were, as Mother said, straight as a board. I can just see me accusing the company of burns all over my body and them asking me if I tried to iron the clothes while I was wearing them.

Manufacturers actually warn you not to curl your hair with a curling iron while in the bathtub. Gee, I thought I'd do it in the shower under my bathing cap.

Fortunately, I've put together so many bookcases that I don't have to read the directions anymore. But I feel sorry for people who do since they were written in China. Thanks to the foreign language programs, our kids will be able to understand the translations, but I have difficulty identifying parts A, B, C and D, and even when I can, I can't figure out which side of the board they're talking about. Everyone knows there's an inside and an outside to boards, but the directions don't address that issue.

One does learn a few things from these verbal and written communications. In bookkeeping, you can't ruminate and numerate at the same time, and in building and operating, you shouldn't read the directions first. Sometimes, it helps if you're inclined to do the things they warn against; you probably will discover that a curling iron doesn't work on wet hair, or that a clothes iron won't smooth out skin wrinkles.

Most of all, we begin to understand that "whaaat" means "you've got to be kidding."

Memories Are For Later

For 60 years, I haven't had time to look back. But the basement is full of five file cabinets of memories, some of which were deliberately preserved, but forgotten. Our family motto was "look forward, never back," but I find that impossible when cleaning out files and I've been ordered to clean the files. Dumping a file without reading every single page would be like selling everything in the kitchen in a garage sale without sorting first.

Perhaps I saved every Mother's Day, birthday and Christmas card I ever received to bask in the sentiments later. Maybe I kept day-to-day journals of every job, notes from every class I ever took or taught, and programs from every event I ever attended to remember later. Maybe I wanted something to do in my old age, but not NOW.

One cabinet is filled with memorabilia from high school. I didn't think paper lasted that long. I notice that I saved only the rewards and good report cards, and that means I had more sense at age 18 than later when the Wyoming Department of Education folders were filled with lurid headlines like "Cotherman Should Resign" or "48-year-old Deputy is Ruthless." I supposed my offspring should know that I had a period of notoriety, but what if the folders leak and end up circulating around my church or somewhere else where people think I'm nice?

The legislative files of the 1980s looked a lot like contemporary ones. We fought because there was limited funding and now we fight because there's too much money. Some legislators seem to have the same attitudes they had 30 years ago, such as lauding women who are willing to walk with the oxen on the Oregon Trail, but punishing the ones who want to drive the wagon. Maybe they'll replace their 18th century orientation handbook this year.

The Wyoming humanities program file was fun to read. What a grand experiment it was to focus the humanities studies on public policy issues. It was quite a challenge having the university's philosophy professor focus the humanities on the Rock Springs water and sewage system. The file contained a few irate letters about showing/discussing horror films. As I recall, we didn't discuss just any old horror film; it had to demonstrate racial, economic, gender or social bias. These films used to be significant films, but the film industry has learned a lot more about violence nowadays, and so contemporary horror films are no longer discussed in academic or any other polite circles today.

The file for the year I worked for the local school district was enlightening. It was my job to organize the first bond issue I ever tried to organize. It was defeated by a few votes, but passed the next year. Partly, that was because I learned that if you tell the whole story (like there will be no kindergartens without more funds), it looks like a threat, and if you don't tell the whole story (like there will be no kindergartens), you lied. In other words, passing a bond is a miracle only free individuals understand/perform.

I love the stuff in the University of Wisconsin file. My job was to get the university research off the shelf and into the public school classrooms where it does some good. We traveled the country eating at really good restaurants, and now I know there's a correlation between hard work/good meals and low reimbursement/debt.

I found every blue book test from middle school to graduate school, and I improved over time. I saved many essays, newspaper articles, research papers and love letters from that same period. I thought if I read them thoroughly, they might provide some clues about my life. They didn't. However, they did enlighten me about writing. The professors either said my writing was too succinct or it was turgid. Even then, I understood that turgidity disguised ignorance, and that if you really knew something, you could be brief because everybody else knew it too.

The files remind us when a paper route was a kid's first job, and we sent him off without a worry unless it was storming, and then we went along or followed behind, discreetly. An anniversary menu reminds us of an elegant Elbow Room where the family went out to dinner two or three times a year and acted like little adults instead of emptying the sugar packets, smearing jelly on the table, or running around screaming.

File folders store many memories and I may not throw them all out. Neither do I intend to visit often simply because the sun doesn't shine in the basement or the attics of our lives. I don't like to visit the sad stories, and it's not necessary to revisit the happy ones because every time I tell them, they get better and better. Indeed, they may not match up with the evidence anymore. Author Cyril Connally said that "our memories are card-indexes consulted, and then put back in disorder by authorities whom we do not control." Thank goodness.

CHAPTER 3

Behind the Veil

It occurred to me while standing in line at the bank near the lobby fireplace that I had spent the whole month getting warm on one side while I was freezing on the other. I kept thinking of Hawthorne's stories with the veiled imagery, i.e., our efforts to disguise the evil with the good. Nothing makes the abstract more concrete than when one side of the body is too hot and the other is still cold. There's the overwhelming realization that this is symbolic of life in general.

As humans, we're a bundle of contradictions. We're the light and the dark, the warm and the cold, the engaged and the disengaged, the happy and the sad. We seem to have two of everything: two arms, two legs, two ventricles to the heart, etc. Thank goodness we were given a sense of humor that enabled us to try to balance the opposites in ourselves. Without the either/or, the rights and the wrongs, we would have no reason to decide, and deciding is what separates us from other creatures. I think, therefore I am.

It's tempting to deny our nature and, instead of engaging in our dialogue, become disengaged and disinterested. Or, perhaps worse, it's easier to pick a single stance and refuse to resolve conflict, either within ourselves or as part of a group.

Maybe if we don't make any choices, if we remain passive, the choices will be made for us. On the other hand, having one answer, no matter what the question, limits our choices too. How do we arrive at the conclusion that the government is not us, but them? How do we view "public" lands, not as land that belongs to all of us, but as "fed" land? It seems to take a lot of effort to balance our one side that seeks to honor each other, and the other that seems fixated only on ourselves.

It perplexes me when people think it's kinder to tolerate injustice than to fight it either in ourselves or others. It confounds me when we refuse to tell a lie, but won't tell the truth, especially to power. It saddens me when we view the objective, and therefore the measurement of life, to be wealth, and then equate wealth with excellence.

When we stand facing the fireplace and the whole front of our body gets too hot while our backside is still chilly and our joints won't bend without cracking, the choice is clear: we back off and change positions. I don't find that easy because it means that I may have to embark into new territories that are unfamiliar and don't feel just right at first. I may not like a heavier jacket or moving faster.

Sometimes it seems harder to find the physical balance than the psychological one. If my mind seems troubled, I just read fiction or biography or history that gives me a perspective that no matter what, humans find their way and even triumph in spite of their complexity and perversity.

By reading and thinking, we understand that we're not the only ones who are a tangle of contradictions. Perhaps out of undue respect for my body, lately, I've been inclined to go to bed early with a heating pad and a good book, and get up early in the a.m. Maybe it's not only possible to be physically comfortable while inviting philosophical discomfort, it's easier to look beyond the veil with warm feet.

Celebrating Age

Spring just happens to be the time when several friends and I celebrate our birthdays, and we have a lot to celebrate. You've heard the expression, "It's no fun growing old" and the counter expression, "Yeah, but it's better than the alternative." Neither of these thoughts are true for us who are lucky, blessed, fortunate. We know it, and we celebrate!

Growing old can be fun, and we have faith rather than facts about the alternative. It's fun because, as a former friend said, we can say anything we want. She perceived this as an indulgence, but it's actually our duty. We must say what others are reluctant to say. And that's reason enough to celebrate.

The fact that we can still be engaged in activities with other people is a cause for joy. That we can walk deserves a large hooray. That we can mow the lawn, shovel snow, scrub floors, or do our own grocery shopping and drive to church makes us very happy. Most of all, that we can climb that mountain and gaze at the entire Laramie Plains or city of Casper and its surrounding plains, gives us a Rocky Mountain high.

A Rocky Mountain high is that wonderful realization that we're only specks on the globe, but the most important life on the planet because, with age, we know we're special, but mortal.

So we give each other birthday cards and consumable gifts and laugh at ourselves and at some of the things people say or do "for" us. We don't really like someone grabbing our arm to help us up or down steps or to walk across the street; we want to grab their elbow and squeeze. We don't really want them to begin a compliment with "at your age," but it's meant to be flattering, so we forgive them and smile.

Sometimes we wish that our bodies and minds were in harmony. That is, if we're disintegrating physically, it might be nice if our minds didn't know it. But we resent it if other, younger people act as if the mind is as decrepit as the body.

My really mature — or exhausted — friends adjust to being invisible and have simply turned to the things they enjoy. They don't try to make a better world anymore because either no one listens or no one cares. If they join anything at all, it's with people who enjoy the same pleasures such as reading, music, art, gardening, sewing or talking about their health.

They're probably wise to do so. Some of us stay engaged because we're stubborn, and that can make life less agreeable. I visit a nursing home about 150 times a year, and I remind myself about what happens when we withdraw (voluntarily or not) from the world. We notice that when we can't care for ourselves, every bit of freedom is removed. We notice that when bodies separate our "selves" from the world, bodies dominate our existence. It's probably this fear that keeps us involved in causes when we should take our minds, hearts and souls to a more selfish place. We don't want our lives and our day's activities based on the most elementary, or should I say alimentary, needs.

We celebrate in spite of the fact that there's a dark side to growing old. We resent the condescension implied in intended kindnesses like being called "honey" by clerks and strange men. We don't like being ignored, but more importantly, we don't like being "humoured." We understand that worse than condescension is having someone roll their eyes at you. Nothing speaks of disrespect more than the eye roll, unless, of course, it's shared with another individual who supposedly also scorns the individual being eye-rolled.

Even the dark side of being old is cause for celebration. It permits us to be testy, outspoken and difficult, and expect the same in return. Patronizing diminishes us, and eye rolling is insulting to both the sender and the recipient. Being old means we can celebrate the fact that we can be what we choose to be. There's a freedom in old age that is rare in our younger years.

And nothing is more celebratory than freedom. Perhaps it's this threat that arouses the ire in the young over the behavior of the old. Or perhaps not. Just don't pop my balloons.

Christmas Favorites

I notice that Casperites are being asked about their favorite movies, books, music, presents, but since no one has asked me, I thought I'd tell you about my favorites anyway. It's my unsolicited present to the few who are still reading on Dec. 23.

My favorite movie, without question, is Dickens' "A Christmas Carol." When I was younger I thought this was a story about selfishness and I liked it when Scrooge (played by Alastair Sim) mended his ways and gave things to everybody. It seemed like the appropriate and wise thing to do after you've been visited by ghosts.

Now I know that Dickens was really trying to dramatize the story of redemption. As my son would say, this is a story that clearly explains no matter how sad your life has been, or how badly you've acted, no matter what damn-fool thing you've done, you can be forgiven and become a new, generous Scrooge. You may, however, need to change your name since Scrooge has come to mean anything but goodness and generosity.

What could possibly top the "Messiah" of all the Christmas music? Feeling all tingly with sentiment will never equal the triumphant uplift one gets from the "Hallelujah Chorus." I long for the hope expressed in "I Heard the Bells," but frankly, it depresses me because we seem so far removed from peace on earth.

The Wyoming Symphony was especially enjoyable this December. I admit that I teared up on "Oh, Holy Night" and I usually don't do that unless I'm listening to Marcia Patton's Children's Chorale; they can move me just by singing "Jingle Bells." We had an abundance of great music this season; I thought "A Christmas Tapestry" was well done, and Carolyn Deuel's "Festival Choir" was outstanding.

The thing about music is that you feel like the human race finally reaches its potential and that it's possible to not only transcend our petty disagreements, but to actually have the wonderful exhilaration that comes with achievement. It gives us hope to realize that the Almighty intended humans to rise above their self imposed limitations.

In books, I admit my favorite is usually the one I've read — or re-read

— most recently, and that is Truman Capote's "A Christmas Memory." It always brings back nostalgic thoughts of my great-aunt who could laugh at anything ... even a flooded basement. I have to admit there are many wonderful Christmas stories ranging from Louisa May Alcott's "Christmas Treasury" to Leo Tolstoy's "Where Love Is, There is God Also."

Though probably unwise to list a favorite Christmas gift, I can't forget a single, short string of blue felt my daughter gave me for my birthday when she was three years old. I wore it on my birthday for years, and on Christmas, too, when I remembered. Last year, Son #1 gave me a calendar with photos of all the children (now near retirement age) through the years. I recalled the years we vied for small children to sleep with because it was so cold at the cabin and they were little heaters. Since then, our rustic cabin has a tin roof, cedar siding, knotty pine walls and new carpet, thanks to the labors of son Bruce and the neighbors in our little valley in the Medicine Bow mountains. The cabin is warm now, but it's rarely filled with laughing family playing Yahtzee, Trivial Pursuit or Pictionary. The family won't play the games that I usually win, even though I give children under four an advantage.

So many of the Christmas rituals cherished by our family grew out of other customs. The tree, the Christmas cards, the lights, the stockings hung by the chimney, yule logs, gifts, tinsel, Christmas Seals and the wassail bowl are all part of American traditions that mostly didn't begin here, but were appropriated and given Christian meanings.

We'd like to think that, born this very season, is the Child that brought grace into this world. But considering our behavior this year, it's always a good idea to begin thinking of resolutions for the new year. It doesn't hurt to try to be worthy of grace. The point is that because there's a Christmas, we don't have to be worthy, but we want to. That's why we're merry.

What's Going On?

Some days it seems that adults as well as children are having a tantrum if they can't have what they want, when they want it. It's perplexing because people generally don't seem to be selfish. In fact, the response to tragedy and catastrophes is overwhelmingly positive.

So what's going on? Are we really into a period of self-centeredness that is likely to destroy us? Why are people doing things like cutting into traffic, going through stop signs, crowding each other at grocery stores, shouting profanities at each other? Why do we seem to be totally unaware of the little niceties that make living together so much easier?

Most of all, what are we doing to our children? Why are we letting them loose in parking lots and other public places, totally unsupervised and undisciplined? Is it because we're lazy? Are we ignorant of the responsibilities of adults and the nature of children?

Why do we have the impression that traditional values of civility have been trashed and that there's no such notion as the "common good"? Why do we act as though we can do what we want, anytime we want, in any place we want, because we're entitled? It's possible that some people feel that this is what freedom means, but it resembles anarchy more than freedom.

So what is it? After a whole lot of contemplation and introspection and several nights of only four hours of sleep, it occurred to me that my own behavior wasn't getting better even though I honored the small and usual rules of community living. I said to myself that if I felt like I'd been minimized as a senior with a limited income in a society that adored youth, money and power, was it likely that other people felt that way too, and, as a consequence, were misbehaving?

What if the prevalent change in our behavior isn't motivated by greed, ignorance or old age? What if change is reflective of our self-centeredness? As my young son said years ago, "Steve is in the way, and I want to be in the way."

Suppose that because we were raised in a country where opinions count, and that we once had some influence, choice and power, we now realize that a few wealthy or powerful people have more influence on our livelihoods, our self-government, the purpose of our schools and even the way we manage our churches and religious beliefs than we do?

What if those who advise us to adapt if our cheese is moved have convinced us that we can't control what's happening to our cheese, our institutions or our lives? In our last-gasp attempts to control our own lives, would it be far-fetched to conclude that if we couldn't control the big things, we could at least demonstrate our freedom by making a choice about everyday things like going through stop lights, invading other people's space, or letting our children loose in crowded parking lots or quiet restaurants?

I should have thought of this sooner. The one abiding characteristic of being 87 is the loss of power. Where once people listened because experience taught us something, old knowledge is now viewed as obsolete knowledge. We've mentioned before that it's this loss of power that makes older citizens ornery, not their loss of mental prowess. Admittedly, it's hard to be impressive if your nose runs and you can't hear or your teeth chatter, but these are physical things having little to do with our personhood. The point is, young people are more inclined to listen to people with fame, youth or money, regardless of their knowledge or experience.

What's really scary is that not only are too many people listening to those with fame and money, but they may be depending upon them to correct the multitude of things that have affected our personal, community, state, national and international lives. That's what happens if we lose our power, or think we have, and make it possible for bad people to take control.

What if we're really acting up because we believe we not only lost our power as free citizens, but have been brainwashed into the idea that we should adapt to it? If our choices disappear, are we really expected to move on and find more cheese or other honey pots? I wonder, like Winnie the Pooh, if we find our treasures, will we be able to squeeze through a very narrow hole to taste them? Or will we figure out what's happening and just say no, you can't move our cheese without our permission?

What Happened to the Middle?

When one of our sons was 16, he wanted to go to a commune in New Mexico for a couple of weeks. Though I didn't consider myself a hovering mother ... after all, I supported his going out in a blizzard to deliver papers ... I said no. His father, however, said that if he would take a bus, he might learn something by going to a commune.

He went, and two weeks later I heard he was back in Casper, but he hadn't come home. The next day he arrived, and I asked where he had been. He said he was at a friend's house cleaning up, and then he glared at me and said, "Do you realize that we're hopelessly middle-class?"

He was right and we still are, but now we may be out of step while 50 years ago, everyone in the block, almost without exception, was middle-class. Evidently, not everyone was hopeless since the culture seems to have shifted to another set of values that we in the middle felt only the "lower" and "higher" classes could get away with.

So, I invite you to mull what it meant to be middle-class. First, it meant that as Americans we were free to become anything we wanted and that the classes weren't permanent, but simply our current circumstances. It didn't matter where we were born, or what "class" our parents seemed to be, we believed that with hard work, good fortune, and some common sense, we could aspire to a better life. It might be a life more prosperous, but it was bound to be a life more satisfying.

We also thought not only could we believe what we wanted, we could say what we wanted and were expected to do so, but nicely. What we didn't believe was that we could DO just anything that we wanted. We were sensitive about what the neighbors would think, and we were convinced that anyone who wasn't lazy could, and should, try to keep up with the Joneses.

We believed that to be successful, we should follow the rules; after all, as Americans, we stood for equality and fairness, and that meant you followed the rules. Those more fortunate in the informal class system (lower/middle/upper) were supposed to be helpful to the "less fortunate," and generally, we were. I recall during the Depression when the family had so little that Mother would piece together and sew coats for us, and that once a month she took food and other clothing to the desperately poor on the Indian reservation.

Middle-class meant that although you might think that the poor were also dirty, you had some empathy for the circumstances they found themselves in. We could discriminate against the dirty and the lazy, but race wasn't the determining factor unless they met the other two criteria.

It isn't old age that makes us want to look back, it's a longing for a gentler society that encouraged us to strive for our better selves.

Being middle-class meant that you changed your underwear every day. One could not risk getting hit by a car and having the rescue workers comment on your dirty underwear. What would the neighbors think? Didn't everyone at the scene of an accident tell every last detail about what they saw?

Being middle-class meant that you mended things. Shoes were re-soled and clothing was mended. Collars were replaced on dress shirts and socks were darned. Everything was also ironed, for a sure sign of being lower class was rumpled clothing. As we grew more prosperous and entered the upper middle-class, I decided that we didn't need to mend everything, but since I decided that before my husband, I found that a mended sock with a knot on the heel, and a shirt with off-center collar tips changed his mind.

Did I fail to mention that the middle-class had three stages since the mobility from middle to lower, or middle to higher was sometimes dependent on outside factors, but not solely based on economics?

If the middle-class is disappearing, as many believe today, it isn't simply an economic calamity, though that is heartbreaking. What should concern us equally is whether the middle-class cultural values are disappearing and being replaced, not by better, more humane, cooperative and caring values, but by a form of individual freedom that is repugnant to a self-governing, democratic, civil society.

Maybe keeping up with the Joneses and caring what the neighbors thought aren't all that ridiculous, and maybe all that darning and preserving could be revived to counter raw consumerism.

Putting On Airs

When it becomes more hazardous to walk on the sidewalk than to travel the Medicine Bow highway in a ground blizzard, I settle in front of my fireplace with a good book and cat naps. Since it's times like these that I convince myself I can just lie around because nobody needs me, I label it modesty and gaze into the flames.

I began recalling stories about public officials I've known over the past 50 years who demonstrated modesty, or at least seemed to in comparison with some of the current "me" generation. Maybe I'm half asleep, but these old-timers seemed to be self-assured, down-to-earth and modest. A few of today's crop of highly placed people seem to be self-delusional and vain. Often, it appeared that the ones in the past who assumed big positions were already successful, so they didn't seek office to become somebody; they were already somebody. Admittedly, if they seemed to have a deep concern about something called "the common good," they may have felt obligated by birth or circumstances to display noblesse oblige.

Sometimes it seems like everybody is working on their "legacy" as though that could wipe out their history. We can't fault people about wanting to leave this earth better than they found it, but wouldn't it be more modest to fulfill that longing as a private, personal goal?

Maybe the old-timers would laugh at the idea that everyone should know what "deals" they were making because when a deal was made, everybody deserved credit. Or they may have kept a secret when they shouldn't. Maybe they knew that the only way to reach a compromise was to do it in a smoke-filled back room where everybody agreed to keep the smoke and the actions to themselves.

The idea of transparency would have been evident in the results rather than the process. But then they might have concluded that transparency has more to do with staging than spontaneous openness. Maybe they thought they didn't have to go out of their way to be vulnerable.

But I digress from flame gazing.

It's possible the jobs kept them humble. Balzac suggests that modesty is a fear of being inadequate, but I don't think so. Those who realized that they'd been elected, not crowned, tried hard to serve the public and the principles they lived by.

I'm sure that if someone today sent the governor daily letters, they would probably get a one-page form return letter created by the public relations person and signed by an administrative assistant, not a short reply on the governor's stationery that said, "Dear Madam: Whatever gave you the impression I am your pen pal?" Signed, "Sincerely, Ed Herschler, Governor of Wyoming."

Other memories of those years in Cheyenne arose from the flames. After serving as first lady, Win Hickey continued to volunteer for government agencies and threw her strong opinions into the discussions. She didn't hesitate to openly complain about the governor's mansion, which she dubbed "that damn ol' drafty pile of bricks" before she moved out, and after.

The officials of old all left a legacy without seeming to try, even though they rarely said "I" instead of "we," unless they were apologizing.

Yep, avoiding those icy sidewalks and dreaming by the fire does cast things in a modest, warm light. Outside, it's frozen with the cold air of vanities.

Remember and Resolve

As I write this just a few days before Christmas, like everyone else, the memories flood in. Most of them are good, and even the lonely ones resulted in something good.

From the experiences that haunt me, however, came the determination to accept Christmas as the most beautiful time of the year and make it happy for my family.

My youngest son told me when he got engaged that he informed his fiancé that she needed to understand that he was going home every Christmas. I trust that was because he loved our family Christmas and not because Mom needed it. My eldest son did refer to it as "Mother's annual production," which may or may not be a compliment.

As it worked out, my youngest son's wife loves our family and enjoys coming home, and the oldest said he admires how the production has evolved into a warm family tradition. He and his wife have recreated a lot of his family traditions and added more of their own including a conference call that includes all family members. My daughter and third son just consider it the day they save for mom, even now, as realization of family became greater than anticipation of presents.

The production started with children baking cookies. These were not the ones I shared with friends since they were usually grey and sticky with sprinkles. There was also the baking of 12 dozen fancier delicacies for the cookie exchange from which we took 12 dozen of someone else's fancy creations that we shared with neighbors and friends.

For many years, when we didn't have a fireplace, we built a cardboard one so we could hang the stockings for Santa to fill. We set out the white milk and grey cookies which Santa/Daddy was glad to eat, even knowing the source.

For a long time it was a tradition to make a recording on Christmas Eve to send to Nanny and Pops. The children read the Bible prophesy and the New Testament, sang carols and then told their grandparents what they wanted Santa to bring. Teenagers went along with young siblings, until the year the smart aleck said, "I hope I get a new jacket" and a surprised mother said, "But you have a perfectly good jacket" and son then said, "But the sleeve is torn and Santa knows you never sew anything."

I still have that recording. You don't send those kinds of messages to a mother-in-law who had only one child and expected you to replace the collars on her son's white shirts and darn his socks. It took some time to figure out how to avoid turning collars by getting them off center and to darn socks by making knots in the heel. No one understood it was the time I might have spent mending the rip in my son's jacket pocket — maybe.

Reading was always a custom at our house, and we read even more at Christmas in order to keep the kids from snooping in the Christmas closet. Books are still part of the tradition, but are now met with the comment, "Is this my used present?" Naturally, I wouldn't give anyone a book I didn't recommend, and I wouldn't recommend a book without reading it first.

I have to thank my mother for making me a reader. She had the unusual technique of chasing me around the house with a broom, swatting and shouting, "You can't read until you finish your chores." When the schools and Casper Star-Tribune make reading a reward for the lap time with a parent or other adult, it seems to work. However, maybe mother's technique would work even better on not only reading, but everything. My mother wouldn't have hesitated to withhold lunch or recess or computers or iPads until the kid could read "Twas the Night Before Christmas" well enough to know it didn't say "and he ran to the window and vomited the sash."

One of the traditions of Christmas, usually connected to the long Christmas list of wants, was an exercise in resolutions. There was enough of my mother in me so that the children not only had to explain why they deserved a new sled, but what they resolved to do next year to be even better little boys and girl.

Of course, I always provided an example. They knew I put losing weight at the top of my resolution list, but when I stopped I explained to them that resolving to lose weight did absolutely nothing to improve the world. Besides when they were little, one son said, "You're not fat, Mommy, you're soft." So I resolved to give a soft response when my mother-in-law called me "my dear." I love connections.

In what I like to call my "later years," I focused on more weighty matters such as poverty, school reform, sex and age discrimination, child neglect, mental illness, nursing homes and promoting music, arts, theater and other food for the soul.

Two years ago, our whole family resolved to stop spending on presents we neither want nor need, and instead contribute to organizations that help the poor, the homeless, the hopeless, the ill and those who need a new start.

It's surprising how much happier it has made all of us. No shopping, we have more time for each other and to count our blessings, and to focus on the meaning of Christmas. Next year, we'll work on giving up any traces of self-righteousness.

I wish you the remembrance of this and past Christmases with joy and gratitude, and the resolve to make it your personal passion to fulfill the promise of Christmas.

Rock On

I must say that I admire the older generation (mine). Sometimes it seems like they have more energy than the youngsters. At least, those who attend senior centers seem to be the swinging generation. Talk about active! Those seniors at the Central Wyoming Senior Center play pinochle, dominoes, bridge, bingo, poker, dance every chance they get, swim, exercise, attend the theater, eat for company and find time to volunteer.

They act as though they're "only old once" (Dr. Seuss) and there's no time to waste. They're doing things their grandparents wouldn't or couldn't consider, and evidently neither would their grandchildren, who spend hours sitting at a computer or lounging with their iPads.

The ones who saved a little when they were younger and had enough sense to inform their offspring that they were on their own after graduating either from high school or college, and the ones who refused to raise grandchildren, are traveling the world to see places they dreamed about between children's orthodontic appointments.

They're dancing to the big bands on Friday night, and lifting weights at 7 a.m. every day. They're better bowlers than they ever were now that they step up to the line and lay the ball down. There's nothing that makes a ball roll straighter and cleaner than not having the strength to hook it.

The same is true in their golf game. The ball may not go far, but it goes straight down the fairway. Fewer lost balls means more funds for luncheons. And since they're over 60, they're forgiven for holding up other old geezers who still play golf because they can afford to.

Although senior tennis games aren't quite what they used to be, the girls still suit up. There are fewer backhand shots, no jumping over the net, and knee-length pants are more prevalent than short skirts that swish. Tennis also provides some good bonding time with younger children who come along to chase the out-of-bounds balls.

Being in that older category myself, I admit there are some down sides to senior status. Indeed, there's very little status outside the senior group. But we admire each other even though we recognize that not all our senses are up to par. So cooking food doesn't smell until it's scorched, and cigarette smoke near the restaurant door doesn't ruin our appetites as it once did.

Hearing is sometimes a problem, but if schools would offer more elocution, articulation and pronunciation lessons, the hearing of the older generation would be quite adequate. It also helps to learn to lip read so that even though you may not hear someone honk at you, you know they have by the shape of their lips.

Food isn't as tasty as it once was. In fact, lots of food tastes like cardboard or sticks in the throat, but fruits go down well, and it's a rare person over 70 who gains weight. It's the first thing a doctor checks, not to see if you've gained, but if you've lost. A few extra pounds mean fewer wrinkles, and so oldsters try to maintain the weight they had when they were 50 and hadn't been bombarded with what was healthy to eat and what wasn't. At a certain age, eating healthy comes naturally since anything really delicious makes you sick.

Large print, prescription glasses and magnifying devices solve most sight problems. I assume that if a person can still drive, they can still read, though not at the same time, as younger people seem to be able to do. It's no longer possible to read more than two books, especially mysteries, at the same time since the plots get mixed up as the memory recedes. It still helps to highlight passages as though you'd be tested in the morning.

Though some senses are diminished, the sense of touch seems to be more pronounced than ever. Animals love to be petted, and seniors find their fur much more comforting than the mink we coveted during our middle years.

As someone once said, "I didn't think I'd get old this fast." That means there isn't a moment to waste in getting all the pleasure that experience tells you will prolong the hours and days. Some people think seniors are complainers, but they're not complaining. They're bragging that they have met life's adversities and survived with added enthusiasm. If you want action, just visit with the 350 people who attend the Central Wyoming Senior Center every week and talk to Wayne Clements about what goes on there. Those seniors and the ones taking OLLI courses give new meaning to "rock on."

Scream Away

If I were choosing a symbol for 2016, I would nominate Edvard Munch's "The Scream." The howling, screaming, moaning wind kept me in the house for four consecutive days … the longest I've stayed indoors since 1984 when I had pneumonia.

It seems like the entire year was about people shouting at each other. Munch drew the picture after he saw blood in the sky. I remind myself that there are screams that are endearing. It's delightful to hear the joyous screams of children sledding down Washington Park hill all the way to Lincoln Street, and the breathless scream of a small child being tossed in the air is welcome.

I've complained about the screams of children in church, but the ones at the early Christmas Eve event were noisy in a creative way in keeping with the season.

The point is, when we're snow- or wind-bound and listening to the moan of the front door and the clattering of the window blinds, it seems like a good time to contemplate the year and sort out the difference between the meaning of scream and the meaning of sad. Maybe after a year of nasty human screams, nature is having the last word and expects us to think about it.

Clearly, any loud noise seems to drown out the soft noise, especially for the hard of hearing. The fact is that when people have hearing loss, they have an increased capacity for listening. We hear the background noise or music on every single television program (except Jeopardy), but not the dialogue. Background noise washes out the message.

That means that screaming washes out the message that might have simply been "pay attention" or "I'm uncomfortable" or "I need something." Oddly enough, crying, which has almost the same definition, actually transmits the same message, but is a gentler way of asking for help and is likely to get an immediate response.

As I looked into the fireplace, I wondered whether anyone had addressed the issue of screaming. My research turned up five references and only two that deserved further contemplation. One said, "His hilarity was like a scream from a crevasse" and I did relate to that, but not for long. The other indicated that "In space no one can hear you scream" and that was fraught with such dreadful meaning politically, I thought I better turn my attention to crying and to my favorite sources: the Bible and Shakespeare.

Both proved to be fertile ground. I found 36 notable and quotable references to cry and crying, and the Bible and Shakespeare expanded the meaning from a physical exercise of the tear ducts to sorrow and supplication. Many are from the Common Book of Prayer and there are many proverbs. None improved my feelings of nature-imposed isolation. Shakespeare was really depressing. I don't recommend King Lear with the wind howling outside: "When born we cry that we are come to this great stage of fools."

But what am I? A child crying in the night (Tennyson)? No, I'm an active book reader and gregarious person longing for discussion. So with the howling rampage outside, I decided to gather books for a January Books and Brew to which I invite friends to take books I've gathered. Since I can't part with more than 100 at a time, it takes hours going through many shelves to select the ones my friends would like, and that I wouldn't trust with casual readers.

It seems like a good way to welcome the new year and say farewell to the old. Screaming is out, and there are positive ways to replace the crying. Or maybe we should redirect it to something bigger than our petty discomforts, like drifting snow. Maybe we could all re-read Alan Paton's "Cry, the Beloved Country."

That's Rude, Dude

After resigning from the school board, I resolved to find some anti-annoyance techniques to deal with the things other people do or don't do. I've since found and now practice a formula that I thought everyone might try, since I'm almost sure these annoyances are universal.

The formula is simple: I find logical explanations for actions that seem insane to me.

For example, does it seem sensible and right to see two people at lunch where one is eating or looking around while the other is on a cell phone? You have to tell yourself that the person on the cell phone is admitting his mother into the hospital and that he's ignoring his table partner because it's an emergency. Obviously, this is an explanation that makes you more sympathetic, doesn't it?

Or maybe you've seen two people at lunch and both are on their cell phones. You have to tell yourself that they're probably talking to each other because they don't really wish to look at each other, or they're on a conference call with the U.S. Department of Education, or the EPA. That's a much more soothing explanation than if you think that two people, two feet apart, talking to each other electronically, is the stupidest thing you've ever seen.

It's also possible that two people at the same table texting each other means they don't want to talk to each other because they're in the midst of a terrible row. This would be a very thoughtful thing to do, since you or I would be embarrassed to hear a screaming fight in a public place conducted by cell phone.

It's possible that people who conduct loud conversations on their cell phones are hard of hearing, can't afford hearing aids and they can't help it. We should be grateful we can't hear the other side of the conversation since this side is boring enough.

Another habit that's a potential blood raiser is when people text during a conversation. I almost got used to this in meetings where no one really wants to hear what anyone else is saying and so, if they're good typists, they can text and look at you and smile as though they heard what you said.

Again, the formula works. These people, no doubt, are responding to the Publisher's Clearing House where they've just won a lifetime income. It's very important in this situation to not alienate this person since you wish to get in line with everyone else for a share of the winnings.

Remember, there are some habits that won't bother us anymore. Things like spitting in the gutter, putting the cigarette out in the salad and picking pockets are almost gone, and taking their place are putting your elbows on the table, eating with fork grasped in the fist and children with piercing screams. These lend themselves to the formula: the individual has a broken elbow and needs to rest it on the table, the individual has permanently bent fingers and must grasp everything with the fist, and the child learned at birth to scream to get attention.

Now that you understand the formula for not being annoyed, we can examine some other troublesome areas. Have you noticed that, except at the pharmacy and bank, people crowd up so close in lines at the grocery or clothing store you could give them a tummy rub? Money and drugs are private matters, evidently, but anything else isn't.

People don't know it, but they need human contact and that's why they stand so close we can feel their breath on the back of our necks. However, they have a tendency to alienate themselves from the person they're with in order to talk electronically to someone else on their list of hundreds of friends.

Remember, computers, phones, iPads , etc., have given us all the opportunity to have immediate friends galore without having to give anything or get anything in return. We just sign up and share things like, we changed our bedding, washed the dog, lost two pounds or something else really significant. No wonder the pushers look for warmth in the grocery line since electronic communications don't exactly transmit warmth.

In other words, my formula allows me tell myself those who appear to do rude things are either needy or can't help it. We could be comforting people who just don't know what 19th century civilized people thought was acceptable behavior in public places. Ignorance is always to be pitied and we must not try to cure it ... not at the child level, not at the adult level. The formula won't work if you expect to change anything another person does or thinks.

The formula only rationalizes the really gauche things people do because they don't know the rules or don't care. But my grandmother said, it's alright to be rude if you do it deliberately and know that you're doing it.

Did I mention my annoyance with people who sing or hum at symphonies or operas? I'm sure they don't know any better, but they think they do, so … well, nothing works all the time.

Greetings or Not

How come the best times seem to be shorter and the worst times seem to last longer? On the other hand, the best times last longer in memory than the worst; probably because we want to remember the best and forget the worst.

The point is, it's only three weeks until Christmas and I still have squirrel-nibbled Halloween pumpkins on the porch, not at all appropriate for Christmas pies, but hardly any time to make fresh ones in any case.

Christmas season should be two months long. Even the church didn't start counting the Advent season until last week. My favorite holiday activity is sending and getting annual greeting cards from friends and that, alone, is a month-long project. First, the greeting can't be written in November; the spirit just isn't there in November. The cards should have been ordered from the Smithsonian or National Geographic, and that couldn't be done in November either because you couldn't make up your mind.

Then you have to sort through last year's cards, and that takes a week or so. Next, the list itself has to be culled, either because someone passed on, the address is wrong, or the addressee didn't send a card for two years and that means they don't like you anymore.

In the meantime, events had to be scheduled around Dec. 1, but you were still trying to determine what to do with the Thanksgiving leftovers. Time must be found for the symphony, all the choral concerts, candle lightings, decorating, preparing chowder and baking a yule log for guests in three short weeks. I have more time since leaving the school board, but it filled in quickly with puttery stuff I wanted to do like clear out files, which had to be read before dumping. Admittedly, my resignation cut the number of cards that had to be addressed since I wouldn't have resigned had I not realized that I only had one friend on the board and that will be confirmed if I receive a card from him. I've crossed out eight names already, and that was before I was through reading the obituaries.

But I digress. This column is about Christmas card greetings. I mentioned that it's wise to save last year's cards. Actually, it's wise to save Christmas cards for about five years so that you can mention grandchildren and great-grandchildren. My friends are sillier about great-grandchildren than grandchildren and offspring because, well, because GGs are darling little people. You can claim that they look or act like their ancestors.

It's also clear that the Christmas letters, including your own, begin to look like last year's. Once the offspring are established, the news is the same unless more clever, handsome children are born. There's also another reason why the letters look the same or have the same news: the news isn't always so good, but the very nature of the season and the reason we celebrate Christmas means the letters need to focus on good news. No negatives are allowed.

All Christmas letters are upbeat, cheerful and exaggeratedly positive. Everybody's kids are clever, over-achieving and well-behaved, or the grown ones are getting high-level job offers, or the old ones are presidents of international companies, have managerial positions, are wealthy or have taken time out to get doctorates.

No one writes or receives a Christmas newsletter that complains about the state of the world, admits that a member of the family dropped out, drank for awhile, was called home from college, was told to go to work or join the Army, has money problems, married someone you don't like, neglected to send a card on Mother's Day, or got fired from their job.

Nevertheless, we look forward to hearing from our friends. They're people we like and who like us even when they know us well enough not to. Newsletter recipients believe every word, or at least pretend to because they really know each other and have learned to read between the lines, and are expected to. You know what it means when they say things like "we just needed some quiet time so I'm in Jamaica and Jill is spending time with her parents, who haven't been well." It's not hard to interpret what "I needed to get rid of my big house, and I'm spending a lot of time with my new friends in this beautiful Assisted Living complex." You accept at face value "Julie wanted to spend more time with me, so I'm teaching her at home."

Friends respect each other's privacy, and they know what you mean no matter what you say. My friends, like yours, have their creative wits together, and don't have to be told that getting old, parenting or having health problems isn't good news.

That's what friendship is all about. There's nothing more cherished than friends, and nothing more deceitful than those who pretend to be. As Shakespeare said, "Friendship is constant in all other things, save in the 'office' and affairs of love."

Only constant friends deserve and write Christmas newsletters, and they're the ones you "grapple to the soul with hoops of steel" (The Bard, again). And isn't that what Christmas is all about?

The Sound of Silence

I have a Native American friend who noted that it was so silent he could hear the sound of smoke on the wind. In the past two weeks I've had a lot of time to contemplate the nature of silence. I've thought about when it's appropriate and when it isn't, when it's comforting and when it's a threat, when it's a vacuum and when it's full of sound.

After attending a sick relative in the hospital for six days, I was surprised to learn that a hospital is the noisiest place in town. Outside the hospital we're warned to keep our speed and our noise at a minimum level, yet in the hospital there's a cacophony of noises ranging from the clanging of bed pans to loud talking by both patients and staff.

When I became snow-bound for two days in a house insulated from the snowflakes and traffic, I cleaned drawers, contemplated and made lists. Since I was thinking about how quiet it was, I decided to scratch out a list of the appropriate and inappropriate places for silence.

Certainly silence is appropriate during an argument between two friends or a husband and wife. Taking sides is ill-advised since friends or couples often end up on the same side against you. Another place I expect to be silent is church. I like to hear only the music and the sermon, and am terribly distracted by shouting or crying children. Ordinarily, I welcome the sound of children, but old habits dictate what I call the "appropriate rule." Relating to sound, the rule is that if seniors need to hear, children need to be quiet.

Will we have quiet traffic soon? When all cars are electric, will those seeking to demonstrate their masculinity find a substitute for loud mufflers? Maybe they could hang something graphic on their bumpers. Scratch that; it's already being done. Perhaps motorcycles could spit fire instead of sound.

What possesses the person sitting behind you in a movie to explain what's happening on-screen? Is it possible that he/she has brought a non-seeing friend and is explaining the action, or a hard-of-hearing companion who wants the dialogue repeated? If so, shouldn't I welcome the explanation of the movie's action as a thoughtful act?

Well, I don't.

When was the "QUIET" sign in the library removed? Even those glued to the computer want to read once in awhile, don't they?

Shouldn't airplane captains give you the choice between reading, sleeping or whispering? Instead of threatening to give you oxygen, couldn't the airline promise a parachute to anyone who talks too much or too loudly? I suppose babies and toddlers have to cry on take-off, but shouldn't there be rented pacifiers that last until landing?

Perhaps the worst noise of all is when every member of a panel discussion decides to talk at the same time. Even with selective hearing, it's hard to sort out one opinion from another when everyone speaks at once. Shouldn't the training for a moderator include interruption skills? On the other hand, maybe a worse noise is silence during what should be a spirited discussion.

It's possible that aversion to noise is caused by shyness, introspection, acute hearing or just plain orneriness, but I don't think so. Even aggressive people react to soft sounds; they shout over them. Soft sounds enable the hard of hearing to nod as though they understand, whereas harsh sounds require a response, best given with passion as though we understand why they needed to be loud. Soft sounds may be preferred, but aren't always welcome; they do require one to listen and that demands a lot of concentration and discipline.

I like some loud sounds such as the peel of church bells when I don't have to understand for whom the bells toll. I love the sound of a singer blasting a high note ... on key. I cry for joy listening to opera.

There's nothing more pleasing than the sound of applause. What could pull one out of the depression faster than a round of clapping? Though it's a sound that confirms our worth, just whistling overdoes it. Stomping and whistling inflates our appreciation and deflates our modesty.

We're told in Revelations that there was a silence in Heaven about a half-hour long. The silence is no doubt for an adjustment after the cacophony of wails accompanying our transition.

I yearn to hear the smoke on the wind, because this sound within a silence helps us drift into imagination. If only we lived in a world where silence is golden and noise is brass. But we don't and so we listen for the silence of smoke as well as a shout of courage.

Defending Liberal Education

There's a quiet revolution going on in education and few people are paying any attention. Those in charge seem to be leaning more and more towards job training ... graduates are to be employable upon graduation from high school, vocational school or college.

Who would argue with the idea that work is important and that there are skills that the young should have by the time they're 18 to 22 years old? But what are the skills?

What brought this all to mind was an invitation from the Wyoming Council for the Humanities to help them celebrate their 45th anniversary. Congress launched the National Endowment for the Humanities in 1965, partly in reaction to the emphasis placed on technology and science, and partly because democracy grew out of the Greek emphasis on a "classical" education in philosophy, literature and the arts.

The programs were launched in 1970 when the National Endowment invited six states to propose state-based public programs. One of those states was Wyoming and I was fortunate enough to be involved as their first executive director.

I just happened to be reading a new book by Fareek Zakaria entitled "In Defense of a Liberal Education," which reinforced my concern about whether humanities studies would survive in a time when the definition of education seemed to be the preparation for work, and the student is viewed as worker. That's a major shift from the idea that compulsory, free education was to prepare individuals for citizenship in a free society, i.e., a society that required an informed electorate.

According to Zakaria, the number of university students majoring in English has drastically decreased. In Wyoming and elsewhere, students are fortunate to read more than one novel a year and are rarely exposed to philosophy, art criticism or history in any depth. In the meantime, there's a grade inflation based, evidently, on the notion that we must praise students regardless of their performance or risk damaging their fragile sense of self-worth.

Though I realize my experience may not be generalizable, I told the

Humanities group this story. When I graduated from the oldest liberal arts college in Minnesota (Hamline University) with a double major in English and history and a minor in psychology, my mother said to me with tears in her eyes, "That's nice, honey, but what can you do?"

Naturally, I responded, "Anything I want to," and Mother admitted later that if a girl is stubborn enough, she probably will do anything she wants to. My point, however, is that Hamline University grounded its graduates in studies that ranged from anthropology to zoology and emphasized daily that each of us owed our talents and abilities to the community.

We came to some understanding through these studies that human beings are complex and capable of the most brutal wrongs, as well as the most transcending and creative actions. Most of all, we learned that we had an obligation to work for the common good.

These notions seem a bit outdated, but the generation that came out of the Great Depression and WWII exhibited a commitment to the idea that the only way to preserve our freedom and be the best of what humans can be was to actively involve and commit ourselves to community.

In other words, we could engage our critical intelligence, but found it unthinkable to demonize those who opposed our solutions. We accepted the idea that the opposition was loyal, and so were we to certain values, traditions and beliefs.

I'm sure that this was the result of a liberal education because I accept the word "liberal" in its original Latin sense "of or pertaining to free men" and the definition of the humanities as specific studies that were considered basic to the preparation of the clergy.

So what are the basic skills taught by the study of humanities? The very skills every school district in Wyoming and elsewhere list, yet leave no time to prepare: critical thinking, creative innovation and problem-solving. Oh, it may take all three of those skills to turn off the sprinkler system, but it's those skills applied to contemplating how human beings live a life of meaning with other human beings that requires more than a manual about how to fix almost anything.

Studies that require thinking, creating, innovating, problem-solving and critical analysis will prepare us for any job we may choose. Americans are doers, but if we look at our history, we also revered thinking. We called it reading, writing and arithmetic, but we also called it science that tried to trace our existence as human beings, and technology that solved a problem rather than created one.

Time After Time

Lately there doesn't seem to be enough time to do things I should do or want to do, so I made a list of what I wanted to do and there would be plenty of days, at least on a daily basis of survival, for what I want to do.

But I'm running out of time for things I should do. If I had only planned ahead more thoughtfully, I could contribute money instead of my time. But I didn't plan well enough and have few funds that aren't already dedicated to something I bought in my self-indulgent years.

So I made a list of what I'm doing with my time. Right on the top is the time it will take to read five books. It's my habit to read them at the same time to suit the mood I'm in. The problem lately is that by dipping into chapters in different books, it's taking forever to finish them.

For example, I decided to read Louisa May Alcott's "Under the Lilacs" again. I must have been eight or nine when I first read it because the language now is dated, even within a nostalgic mood. John Dos Passos' book, "The Shackles of Power," is putting me to sleep, whereas Diane Ravitch's book, "Reign of Terror," slows me down because what she says is so true, I have to write notes. That leaves "The Queen Mother" by Lady Colin Campbell, which I'm tempted to quit reading because it smears the Queen. But it's kind of juicy, so I'll read one more chapter or jump around to see if I can find any other bit of character assassination.

I'm eager to begin the new book by Alexander McCall entitled, "Sunshine in Scotland," and I'm still dipping into Edgar Allen Poe's "Mystery and Imagination" since a) it's the month for goblins, and b) I won a declamation contest by acting out "The Telltale Heart."

So if reading remains at the top of the list and some time is reserved for writing and my OLLI class, what needs to be omitted farther down on the list? My twice- or three-times-a-week visit to Shepherd of the Valley? That's not a burden .. that's my daughter-in-law.

How about the Seton House board? They provide housing and help with education and jobs for single parents. That's a possibility; we can find a younger, more energetic person to take my place. Maybe Joshua's Storehouse could use someone else, but I've always been dedicated to food and families, and they pack food for families every day.

I could resign the Vestry at St. Mark's Episcopal Church. Indeed, there may be a few sighs of relief if I do. But I'm at the age where I'm preparing for the next move and have no intention of alienating the landLord.

That leaves politics, which just raises my blood pressure, so that's a possibility, and there are committees connected with every board where they ask you to do things and then ignore what you've done. I may move that to the top of the list of possible time savers.

Swimming takes two or three hours a week, and although it means that my shoulders or legs ache all the time, the water is soothing. Since I can't wear my hearing aids in the water, it's also a quiet time of week.

There are too many problems that need to be addressed and time after time, women of my generation were reminded that we must be good citizens and community volunteers while men were making money.

Time doesn't change old habits until it runs out.

Waiting

I've always been an impatient person. Waiting in line frustrated me; waiting for an elevator annoyed me; waiting for someone to finish a sentence exasperated me. The only time I managed to be patient was when my children needed me to be.

During the past two weeks, however, I acquired a different view and respect for patience. On Jan. 10, my daughter-in-law was hospitalized with pneumonia. Since she has suffered from MS for several years, the prognosis wasn't good.

After five days in the hospital, her husband (my son) decided to take her back to the nursing home where she had resided for three years, and arranged for hospice care.

Though we had spent most days with her, we began attending her around the clock. Her son arrived from Ohio and we sat with her and counted the moments by her labored breaths.

Though we longed for her release, we found that patience may be rooted in an eagerness to hold back the inevitable. We didn't want her to suffer, but we didn't want her to die. We wanted her to shed the body that had prevented her from riding in the dog sled races, cross-country skiing, hiking or gardening, but we wanted her with us forever.

We regret that she hadn't been able to grasp the nanoseconds of pleasure that her immobile life provided: a feeble joke, a fresh bouquet, a manicure, a book on tape. News of family weddings, new jobs and trips didn't help her feel better, but simply reminded her of all the things she could no longer enjoy.

So, we waited while she and God decided when it was time. We tried to hold back the time as though there isn't a time for everything and everything is in its time. She died on Monday and we have no doubts that her new life will suit her better than the one she endured for the past few years. We know she won't have to be patient with either the physical pain or the agony of an inactive life totally unsuited to her temperament.

As for her family, I suspect that we each have acquired some small wisdom. What was a blessing for her is hard to be viewed as one for us since we, like Phyllis, wanted to turn back the clock. We, too, wanted to keep her as she once was — vital, active, stubborn, head-strong and fun — knowing that was not to be. We wanted to, but couldn't deny the rhythm of existence; nothing happens before its time, no matter how we try to alter it.

We may not like life's cadences, but we do have the choice of waiting in anticipation rather than annoyance. We do have the choice of catching the little moments of pleasure and wonder. Our Phyllis died under a full moon and the planets were aligned in welcome. She no longer waits, nor do those who loved and cared about her.

CHAPTER 4

Backward or Forward

It's been awhile since I thought of palindromes as a symbol of life's experience. Overall, backward is forward, and forward is backward.

Words that repeat themselves triggered my admission that in my senior years, there's little difference between beginnings and endings. For example, does it matter what one intends if we regret it? I've noticed that in the present culture, explaining our good intentions is supposed to wipe out our mistakes, and the regrets seem to have more to do with being sorry we made a mistake than in apologizing for the mistake itself. After all, the logic seems to go, if we mean no harm, then surely no harm was done. And so, intent and regret are companions. Forward becomes backward.

If you think about it this way, there isn't a big gap between foresight and hindsight. With a little courage, it's easy to predict the outcome before it happens, and it takes slight memory loss to claim afterward that you knew it wouldn't happen. If your prediction turns out to be false, in retrospect you can explain that had circumstances not changed, what you predicted would have happened, or you can claim you never said it would.

For example, I know that breakfast will burn if I leave the kitchen and begin watering plants, but I certainly can say, after putting the fire out, that I had both foresight and hindsight. I acted with brilliant foresight and rational hindsight when I chose to water plants so that I could put the fire out.

In education, we concentrate on the word "focus" frequently. If we could only get someone to focus, we say, the organization would be more effective and the student would be more successful. Yet it's the random thought that creates something new and the exploration that leads to innovation. Full cycle, when focus joins forces with random thoughts, we still get results, so did we begin with focus or random thoughts? The end or the beginning?

Last week I began a search for clothes to go to the dry cleaner. In short order I began going through closets, drawers and boxes to cull those in good condition to sell or give away; then I began sorting those that go to charity, and discovered some just needed to go to the laundry. Finally, the really outdated ones were saved for squares to make a quilt. Now all I have to do is find a quilt maker because I meant to sort quilting material when I started, didn't I?

I like words that spell forward or backward because they represent the life cycle. It's a major discovery to find that kayak, deed, civic, noon and solos read the same from left to right and vice versa. Maybe they're there to remind us that if we had to live our lives over, we would probably repeat ourselves.

It's no mystery that the over-70 crowd inserts memory stories into every conversation. These are the stories that freeze the impatient young person into a glassy-eyed statue. They know we do it, but we just can't stop because we have a duty to demonstrate that the past is prologue to the future. Beginnings are endings, forward isn't different from backward, intending is similar to regretting, foresight is hindsight. Besides the responsibility of passing on their wisdom, older people have vivid recollections of 50 years ago that they need to recall while they try to remember what they had for breakfast, or whether they had any at all. We don't tell stories because we want to, but because we have to test whether the mind still works. If the below-60 crowd understood this, they would be ever so much more tolerant of why every event, occasion or idea reminds oldsters of a story from their past.

Name a topic. Economic downturns? Did I tell you about the summer we only ate macaroni, tomato and onion salad? I did? Did I say it was 1939? Oh. Did you know my brother, your uncle, was in the good war? The newspaper showed a map of his progress from Normandy to Berlin as his company rushed to get there before the Russians. I told you many times? Well, it bears repeating.

Did you know I lived through the McCarthy era? What do you mean, who was McCarthy? He was an egomaniac disguised as a congressman Communist hunter. My mother-in-law ordered me to get out of the League of Women Voters because McCarthy's buddy, Fulton Lewis, said the LWV was a commie dupe. I think looking over one's shoulder during this period probably has something to do with our lifelong back problems, so beware. Fear is the result of evil and its cause and another example of not knowing whether it's coming or going.

Today's morals are deplorable! Let me tell you what was considered unethical if not immoral in 1947. Doing a take-off on the Gettysburg

Address in the student newspaper would get you a trip to the principal's office. "Four score and seven years ago our fathers and mothers brought forth in this world, darling children conceived in passion and dedicated to the proposition that all men are created evil." I was personally connected to the girl who was mortified when the mild-mannered principal asked her how she knew she was created in passion. I didn't talk about passion for years, and squirm to this day if someone says I have a lot of passion, even if they're talking about ideas.

So study palindromes to fully grasp that beginnings and endings are one and the same. A madam is a madam, a deed is a deed, and poop is poop. And today's events happened before. That's why it's more fun to be with young people since they don't know yet that they'll be able to envision their lives backward. And that makes us feel better about not remembering why we're standing on the patio with a spatula in hand.

Un-resolving Changes

I'm pondering whether to make any new resolutions for 2015. The problem is that I know I'll have to deal with a multitude of changes, unbidden and unresolved, and it may be foolhardy to deliberately take on more.

But I shall, if only to prove that the notion that older people can't change is a myth. Indeed, we oldsters can demonstrate that we have to change daily and are transparent and accountable about it, which is more than one can say about those who make secret resolutions that no one knows exist, let alone carry out.

Older people appear to be "set in their ways" simply because they sigh and shrug a lot while they're changing.

For example, when I wake up in the morning to a cool room, but toasty bed, I really long for that big, neck-to-toe stretch, but, as age advances, every time I stretch I get a cramp somewhere. That's a big change, regardless of whether it's a resolution.

There was a time when eight to 10 straight hours of sleep was normal; now normal is two trips to the bathroom in a six-hour period, one of which is at 4:30 a.m. and inevitably becomes the normal time to get up. I doubt if people under 60 ever resolve to get up at that hour unless they wish to see the sunrise coming up over a lake or mountain or they haven't gone to bed yet. They never, however, make a habit of actually rising at 4:30 a.m.

Remember when you were a kid and laid on the grass just looking at the sky? Older people have had to give that up for a couple of reasons. First, because if they don't keep their eyes on their feet, they risk falling and breaking their necks, arms, legs or other body parts. And second, because it isn't easy to get down and almost impossible to get back up. If anyone thinks this isn't a huge change in how we navigate, try walking with your eyes closed, a lame leg and two glasses of wine to replicate our normal agility.

Seniors have to change more than anyone else, and it's outrageous to suggest we're incapable of change. It's simply that sometimes, we long to change back to where we were before alien customs and ideas were thrust upon us.

Think about how the body itself deteriorates. Why would anyone over 60 not wish to shower with 18-year-olds before diving into the pool? There's nothing like a bathing suit and an appalled teenager to want to change our desire to swim. The young will change their minds about old bathers once they realize that all bodies disintegrate sooner or later, but it will be too late. They're already being pulled by gravity.

Most of us seniors aren't afraid of change, we just don't like the direction it's taking. Change should gently return us to our best of times, not throw us forward into a chaotic world. It doesn't seem like too much to ask that life be an upward spiral rather than a downward plunge.

Changes of the mind are mostly positive. With a lifetime of experience, the mind alerts us immediately to dishonesty and fakery. Remember when we'd tell our kids that we knew because a little bird told us? Well, it's true as we grow older. The bird may be called intuition, but we can discern things that were completely overlooked when we were young.

We can tell a lot about motives simply because we went through the stages of bad motives ourselves, like aiming to be attractive, wanting to be rich, yearning to be important. Now we simply hope to be living.

We admire the young when they value freedom, but we believe that freedom's twin is responsibility. Our parents had no hesitation about demanding that we carry in a cord of firewood before we got to play. We don't understand why any demand on a child or adult is viewed as a threat to their sense of self or their freedom. A change backward could be good.

I began reading books on the Salem Witch Trials during my experience in state government. Now there's a welcome change: women aren't hung anymore for not tucking themselves into the molds they're supposed to, even though they're hung out to dry all too often if they're "feisty," i.e., assertive.

I can't help but wonder what would happen if we resurrected the habits of the past for public schools. Can you imagine dress codes, principals who give swats and parents who treat teachers like professionals? What would happen if children were kept back until they learned what they were capable of learning?

As for me, I resolve to change back to the values I cherished and the body I coveted, and like anyone else, I'll consider it a great new year if I achieve even half of the changes, resolved or unresolved.

Comfort, Comfort

Well, elections are over and we can once again turn our attention to principles and other high-minded ideals. It's an appropriate time to turn our thoughts to the simple events, places and people that help us all transcend our shabby selves.

Sitting on top of Cooper Hill west of Laramie has always made me feel like both queen of the world and the most insignificant speck on its face. There's something about listening to the wind soothing the limber pines, and the view of the deer meandering out of the forest copses where the snow melts and cuts a groove in the mountain, that comforts me. On top, 8,400 feet up, I celebrate my journey even though I realize it was easier to climb up it than it will be to climb down.

Another place I always feel comfortable and even inspired is a college campus and classroom. There are some places one just seems to belong, places you can relax and express yourself without alienating anybody. Indeed, self-expression is encouraged and challenged, and a community is formed.

I get a similar feeling speeding over the boundary waters between Ontario and Minnesota. I identify with those brave explorers who guided their birch bark canoes or pelt vessels through vast, unknown and unpopulated waters. How did they know they would reach land again? How did they climb up those bare cliffs that sliced through the water to draw pictures on them? There, dozens of miles out on a small island, a man, comfortable in his sense of the future, built a two-story log castle for a bride who never came.

No matter how annoying other people's children who disrupt my quiet dining have become, I get an overwhelming feeling of contentment when my own grown children and grandchildren are all in my living room or at the cabin, telling stories that make fun of Mother and life, and recall the pleasure of growing up in a neighborhood where the mothers ritually drank coffee together while children played and fought. Everyone took comfort that others would not only discipline their kids if they needed it, but were expected to do so.

I wonder why we can feel a great sense of community in a symphony concert or in a high school auditorium viewing a high school musical. Maybe, for just a couple of hours, we take comfort in what young people are capable of being and doing when adult and peer expectations are high. Why do we get a sense of community at a crowded symphony where we don't even have elbow room, yet feel alienated at the grocery store if someone invades our space at the checkout counter?

Is there any greater sense of well-being and comfort than sitting in front of the fireplace with a cup of tea and a good book? Indeed, it feels good to just sit there, watching the flames and contemplating the goodness of life and of people.

Why are we in such a hurry? It takes time to seek out the experiences that help us transcend our dark sides. What sparks a trip from the dark to the light?

How come we love motorboats and cars, but hate computers? How come some of us enjoy dinner parties, where people share their politics, religion and psychological problems, but rebel at public meetings where we're asked to tell how we feel and confess our most embarrassing moments?

In the television world, one would think that all discomfort is physical and can be treated with yet another pill. But our comfort has to do with things that soothe our minds and spirits, and have little or nothing to do with our physical well-being. If it was physical comfort we seek, we wouldn't climb mountains; we wouldn't risk capsizing on the boundary waters; we wouldn't expose ourselves as social misfits on a college campus or in a classroom; and we certainly wouldn't feel good as the butt of our children's laughter.

Admittedly, comfort has two sides. Walking in the rain or snow is contentment; driving in it isn't.

An arm offered in crossing the street, not the hand that grabs the elbow, fills us with comfort and warmth.

Linen tablecloths, candlesticks and silver goblets make soup taste like filet mignon, but eating filet mignon while watching middle eastern refugees doesn't taste good at all.

A room filled with books is comfortable; a room of knickknacks isn't.

"Two loves I have of comfort and despair," said Shakespeare. He doesn't mention that one is an antidote for the other, but I do. Comfort sweetens our despair.

I Go To the Hills

It's time to go to the parks and the hills to revive all our senses that are dulled by familiar spaces, sounds and smells. It's time to get outside.

It's true that during a howling blizzard and cold, high winds, we appreciate that protected feeling close to the fire or simply within the shelter of our homes, but even books and the internet pall after awhile, and we need to explore the natural world of squirrels and other living creatures.

Fortunately, Casper has a variety of public parks and a mountain to explore. What foresight our local, state and federal founders and current leaders had in saving spaces for all the people, not only in Casper, but in Wyoming. I live below Washington Park, which offers not only a view of the city, but the sounds of birds, animals, dogs, children at play and band concerts.

Hundreds enjoy the concerts and watch and listen as the sun disappears in a sky of amber over the hill and the whole world seems to float on a breeze to a Sousa march or a heartfelt rendition of "America the Beautiful." There's nothing quite like a Wyoming summer evening at an open band concert.

In between concerts I walk my dog. A few years ago, I took a bag along to pick up refuse, but I stopped that once I had to hold on to a cane with one hand and the dog leash with the other. Or maybe I stopped the day two little girls pointed at me and said, "There's that bag lady right now." I walked City Park the day JFK was shot, and I walk Conwell Park during the Christmas lighting. I always think what a treat it must be for those in hospital rooms across from the park; I know I always feel like a kid when the Christmas lights are turned on.

Our family is especially fortunate in having a cabin in a valley behind Cooper Hill outside Laramie. I test my age each year by climbing to the top of that hill, above the Laramie Plains. It seems to me that in my 70s, it only took about 30 minutes to get to the top and now it takes an hour or so, and even longer to get down. I zigzag more because I don't want to roll down like an Indian rubber ball, even though I notice that my grandchildren seem to always walk directly below me as though to break my fall. I'm determined not to fall, no matter how long it takes.

I need to get to the summit, however, to renew my perspective after a long winter of discontent. As I sip my thermos of coffee and view the plains for miles and miles, I'm in awe. The wind has blown all the branches to one side of the limber pines and I suppose that is why they call them limber. I can hear the pine's main limb saying, "Well, you're here now and there's no going back, so make the best of this view" or something like that. I imagine that tree limbs, like all living creatures, actually communicate to each other. Or maybe it's just the wind.

A few deer wander out of the copse of trees in the gentle ravine below, and they munch on the grass every now and then. They look at each other and comment on what a nice day it is and I wonder if they know enough to enjoy themselves before the shooting starts in the fall. They probably savor the moment far better than we humans do.

I can spot the monument of a grave near I-80 just as the highway climbs into the hills. Wyoming historian Al Larson told me that it was the grave of a remittance man. A remittance man was the second son of British aristocracy sent to Wyoming, often to ranch. Because he wouldn't inherit the estate in England, he received a monthly check from home. I think it's romantic to believe that one of our senators was a remittance man.

Sometimes at sunrise, I sit on the deck facing the east to watch the sun peek up over Cooper Hill. I know it's coming, but I always watch in anticipation and wonder as it creeps over the hill to drench the grass and aspen and beaver pond in our little valley with golden light. The rock chucks see it and move, and the hawks fly down from the hill to snatch the baby bluebirds in first flight.

At night, we turn off all the lights and sit under a blanket of stars. We don't need the telescope, but are even more enchanted by the stars and planets that hide themselves in the city sky. We wonder if there are other "humans" out there somewhere and if they know we're here and what they think of us. And we're convinced that surely this universe can't be accidental.

Summer is when we reconnect by walking in the park, viewing the world from a mountain somewhere, or digging in the soil. We should outlaw summer meetings, and church should be held in a park.

I go to the hills for the sound of my soul at rest.

Capstones and Milestones

It's graduation time and if I had been asked to speak, I would have said the following:

Though you're feeling relief, pride, anticipation and fear, I hope you realize that graduation isn't a capstone, but a milestone. You may think it's the end of something; it isn't. You'll need to be a lifelong learner if you want to survive.

Some of you may have simply been marking time by using your brains to send clever messages by computer, hanging out at the mall or talking your parents into buying you a motorcycle or at least a mountain bike. It took some intelligence to convince both the teachers and your parents that you were giving all your efforts to their expectations while pursuing your own. I know about these things because I have an excellent long-term memory even when I forget where I put my glasses.

Well, if you think you can keep doing your thing rather than theirs, you're bound to get long stories from your parents and others about how it was when they were growing up. Remember that a milestone means you've just finished part of the course. Understand that your parents and grandparents are looking at their milestones in retrospect, and while they realize that the longer they live, the less they know, they'll never admit that to the younger generation.

The fact is that every generation that preceded you was remarkable, or so they say. They had better values, they were more ambitious and they were honest to a fault. They relied a lot on something they called common sense because they didn't understand scientific inquiry. They trusted hero politicians because they glorified the system. They believed that things happened for the best, and that faith is believing in something that hasn't been proven and doesn't need to be.

I hope you have common sense, but you'll need a few other skills. So I hope you've learned to think creatively, and I believe you have since many of you outsmarted your folks by doing little or nothing related to school. However, you probably learned to figure out a whole lot of things that school would never teach you. For instance, you learned how to solve problems yourself because you didn't want your parents to know that you had a problem. You learned to take the initiative when you had to figure out how to do what you were instructed not to do.

You may or may not have learned problem-solving, critical thinking and creativity in the classroom, but you probably learned these things "on the street" as the expression goes. The good news is that the "street," i.e., life, is where you'll continue to learn. Truth is, we learn by doing, and that can be gratifying or painful. Some of the things you learned in class will help you have fewer mistakes ... maybe.

Our generation finds it annoying when you think you know more than we do, even though we admit that the six-year-olds in our families have to explain to us how to get the computer to do what we want it to do, and that our 16-year-olds often spot political phonies before we do.

In fact, it may be this realization that you know more about the environment, human relations (especially sexual), the body (especially how to keep it healthy) and how to get your way with adults, that makes us so eager to tell you how it used to be but wasn't, and how well-behaved we were when we weren't.

What we don't want to admit is that the graduating class of 2016 is much more flexible than we were. You expect things to change because you've already seen the family's structure change, communications expand, economics transform, and the community evolve. Regardless of what skills and knowledge you may have or what jobs or careers you take now or after further schooling, you'll probably change directions four or more times during your lifetime.

Although I loved literature, history and several other studies such as psychology and anthropology, and hope that you did too, I admit that skills I learned and have used forever were acquired from non-credit activities such as school declamation and theater, chorus, research, writing, student government and waitressing.

If you were fortunate enough to learn from mistakes both at school and at home, you have a head start on getting to the next milestone. From what I've observed, you'll make it because you've got our number. When you realized that learning was something you could control, you did so whether it was inside or outside the classroom, and when you learned that you could "con" adults by giving the least effort to their expectations and the maximum to yours, you learned to differentiate between the abstract and concrete.

When you figure out why pre-K-12 education was mandatory and free, you'll realize that whatever you learned is to be applied to the many facets of your life, as a mate, parent, citizen and worker. Our generation hopes that you continue to be critical of "old" ways and that you propose and preserve better ways. It isn't as though we gave you a model you'll always want to emulate.

One of your ancestors did give us a pathway for the rest of our lives. He said that if we believe we can remain ignorant and free, we believe what never was and never will be. So when you don't want to think or act like us older folks, we ought to be optimistic. You'll need to think independently if you're going to keep growing.

This graduation is your personal milestone, not a capstone; that takes a lot of living.

Don't Fence Me In

I just added another annoyance to my list: people who crowd you in the checkout line at the grocery store. They seem to stay behind the sign at the bank and the pharmacy, but they get right up to your elbow at the grocery store.

I'm friendly to strangers; I talk to them in doctors' offices, department stores and, yes, grocery stores, but I don't want them in my space while I'm writing a check or using a debit card. It's bad enough that they know at a glance that I'm a chocoholic and like Brussels sprouts, but why must they peak at my name, address, telephone number and account number on my check?

Those are the practical reasons I don't want someone standing beside me or looking over my shoulder when I'm conducting business, but that's simply a mental annoyance. What I feel, however, is similar to what you'd feel if someone asked you to lick their spoon. Their physical presence is repugnant to me. There's a space around us that mustn't be violated, with or without signs. You don't enter someone else's house without knocking. You don't review someone else's mail unless invited to do so. You don't borrow someone else's clothes without permission, and if you do, we protest. What do you do when someone seems to be close enough to wear your jacket?

Where's their sense of privacy? Why do we want the "feds" to stay out of our business, yet move into a stranger's territory? Is it because they announce all their personal thoughts on Facebook or Twitter? Is it because they feel so isolated, they seek out the warmth of another human being, even a stranger? There's no doubt that many people reside in intellectual bubbles, surrounding themselves with the stale air of opinions they've already inhaled. Maybe they think you have a bubble, too, or aren't there.

Why, then, do they bump their bubbles against mine? Is that person standing six inches from me immune because his life is a reality show and he isn't really there? Is he accustomed to being alone or afraid of being alone? The fact is, there's nothing as lonely as being in a group ... at least some groups. Maybe he's withdrawn from groups, or believes that groups actually share space ... and he doesn't wish to share space.

Whatever the explanation, it's strange to live in a state that has miles and miles of uninhabited space only to be crowded in a grocery line or any other line that doesn't have a sign that says "Wait here until called."

One of my favorite pastimes is reading about historical figures, and one of the characteristics I remember in reading about Lyndon Johnson was that he tended to get in his colleagues' faces. He evidently could persuade his Senate colleagues to pass bills he favored by grabbing their lapels and breathing in their faces. I thought he was the height of rudeness. I now believe that people agreed with him just to remove him from their space.

I've tried to be polite, but indicate that someone in line should back up a bit by saying things like, "I'll be finished here in a minute" or "I'm not done yet." That only works with someone who mistakenly wanders into my space because he's just come from a funeral. The only command that usually gets a reaction is "back off." It usually isn't the reaction I seek, however, and my son discourages that since he worries about concealed weapons. I don't, because so far anybody who invades my space is close enough for me to know whether he's carrying.

There are, of course, other ways that people invade your space without physically crowding you. Instead, they ask questions that are none of their business. Many of them take pride in knowing who's related to whom, whether they're having troubles with their mates or children, and how much they're rumored to have in their bank accounts. These intruders aren't as annoying because we don't have to physically remove them from our space. We simply remove them psychologically by not answering their questions, unless we're feeling frisky. Then we give them fictional information to see how far it can be distributed in an hour or so. That isn't as much fun as it once was now that we understand how disastrous it can be.

So whether on the street or highway or in line at the store, back off. It's the polite thing to do, and you get where you're going just as fast ... especially if you don't provoke a confrontation.

Being Left Behind

Do you ever have the feeling that there's a connection between all of the events that happen in a short space of time? I've had that feeling about the past two weeks.

First, my daughter finally moved to Laramie after weeks of work preparing her house for rent or sale. I thought I'd be relieved, but there's this awful sense of abandonment. Then our OLLI writing class tried to distinguish between sentiment and sentimentality, empathy and self-pity in order to identify good writing, just when I was about to launch a pity party.

Next, the 51-year-old son of my long-time friend, Lynn, died after three weeks of illness. What greater catastrophe than to have a child die before the parent? I know many people over 70 who, though grateful to be alive, would prefer to die before their children do.

Everything seemed to add up to the gut feeling of being left behind. Like our pets, we'd rather go than stay. It occurred to me that if we entered the cave of abandonment, we could lose the light we needed to differentiate the mildly sentimental from the maudlin, or empathy from self-pity.

I asked myself and the class if the feeling about being left behind is a genuine factual sentiment or a way of indulging in self-pity? Is the event about us or about someone else? We aren't sure about the characteristics of sentimentality, but we know it when we see it. Sentiment seems to be directed outward and sentimentality inward. Literature is about us, death is about us and being left behind is about us, so maybe it's a matter of degrees.

We can see it in other people's writing or actions, but how do we see it in our own? What, we may ask, are the warning signs? When in doubt, make a list of things we once did but can no longer do, if we want to go on rather than be left behind.

Your list will be unique to you, but here's the idea. It's important to print, number and post them.

1. When your family leaves, stop shopping at Sam's Club unless you wish to buy huge quantities to share with Joshua's Storehouse

or the Cross Roads Kitchen.
2. Go ahead and purchase all the books or other indulgences you want. You don't have to hide them since family members living elsewhere wont know you haven't had them all along.
3. Install a railing on the stairs, but walk up and down as often as you like without holding on.
4. Adopt another 55-year-old to nag you about walking up and down stairs.
5. Find a young friend to help with garage sales and to have tea with on Sundays.
6. Wear the same clothes two days in a row since only a family member would tell you that you smell musty.
7. Charge your cell phone periodically so that you can be rude to sales people daily and get weekly calls from sons or daughters.
8. Loudly criticize politicians, traffic violators, neglectful parents and poor-performing elected boards without fear of embarrassing a member of the family.
9. Go to places that bored the person you miss, like lectures and the mall.
10. Encourage friends to tell you when you're mawkish, overly-sentimental, cloying, saccharine, schmaltzy, weepy or hokey so that you can criticize them for having little or no compassion anymore.

If you have trouble seeing the connections between literature and sentiment, death and life, going and staying, just make a list anyway. Being left behind is a little like being in the way; the choice is ours.

Lighten Up

St. Mark's is having a gong show. Episcopalians believe that those who embarrass themselves together, stay together. Besides, we're known to have all the pageantry and none of the guilt (according to Robin Williams). The point is that giving silly performances and risking rejection builds community.

It takes a bit of courage since I still recall the experience of being in a neighborhood audition for "Major Bowes Amateur Hour." It was something like American Idol; amateurs had a chance to be on a national radio broadcast, but if they weren't very good, an oriental gong would hasten them off stage. My three older cousins decided to try out and they thought that if they added cute little me, to sing, to the trombone, trumpet and sax, they might win. It took a lot of chocolate bribes to get me to practice, and they blamed me for losing. I believe it was their bad trumpet note and not my mouthful of chocolate that got us gonged, or it could have been their choice of "The Music Goes Round and Round and it Comes Out Here."

Their mother, my great-Aunt Grace, sided with me. She thought that they picked on me just because I had tattled on them. In retrospect, she indulged me and that's why my mother wouldn't let me stay there longer than two weeks at a time. But then my mother wouldn't have laughed, as Aunt Grace did, when we got the gong. Mother would never have thought that being rejected was an incentive to practice more or find other ways to get chocolate.

Aunt Grace had what the world needed in those Depression years, and today. We especially need to laugh at ourselves. Surely some of the candidates for president go home at night and laugh with their mates about some of the things they've said that day. If they don't, this is serious and Shakespeare was right: the line between the sublime and the ridiculous is getting extremely thin.

The thing about humor is that it has to be a way of forgiving ourselves for being flawed but wonderful. Think about it. We're the only one of God's creatures that's capable of laughing at ourselves. Hyenas or gorillas don't count because their laughter is reflexive, not reflective.

We need silly skits, off-key musical presentations, bad poetry and funny last words and epitaphs to remind ourselves that we were never expected to be perfect, and that it's OK to be cheerful about it. Besides, it's better to make a fool of ourselves than to have others do it for us.

So we read the comics every morning because they remind us to laugh at ourselves. We could use a new Will Rogers to deflate our balloons of self-importance. Maybe, if we try, we could revive modesty as the foundation for self-derision.

I wonder whether the growth of virtual reality has helped us lose touch with our inner souls. Surely, there's a certain risk in experiencing things virtually rather than really. Is the next step experiencing life by experiencing real happenings through head pieces that connect us with the world, but separate us from the person standing next to us?

If we don't know what to take seriously, how will we know when to laugh? If someone asks you how to improve their bowling game and you tell them they might make more strikes by throwing the ball underhand rather than overhand, we must presume that this is a concrete impossibility or it's not funny. Bad example, but at least the anxious bowler didn't seek my reassurance again.

What seems to be missing currently is a common understanding of what is ridiculous and what isn't. Is falling from the roof funny? Will Rogers said that everything that happens to someone else is funny, and so there are shows like "America's Funniest Videos" that show people being hurled about. Personally, I don't find them funny, but there are many people that don't find Oscar Wilde's comedy of manners like "The Importance of Being Ernest" funny either.

Humor has to be rooted in truth, and a gong show invites people to laugh at themselves by putting an act together that's based on a serious human experience but makes it laughable. As for me, it was an opportunity to trace the progress and regression of growing old in order to demonstrate how silly it is to expect to do so with dignity.

It may be hard for those at the 50-yard line of "growth" to understand that the further one goes along that continuum, the more appreciative we are of how funny life is. While it's true that some of the things that happen to the body, such as stiff joints, unsteady balance, finger and leg cramps, etc., aren't very amusing, one's sense of the silliness of human behavior is sharpened.

Aging frees us of the pretensions associated with ambition, self-importance and control, to laugh at ourselves with a degree of affection that we never could early in life. We're free to say, and do, and be and accept, even be comforted by the notion that we did the best we could with the natures we were given or acquired.

The joke, dear ones, is on us. God expects us to die laughing.

The Rest of the Story

Mother's Day was one of the best I've ever had. Since it was snowing, blowing, raining and sleeting, my daughter and I played cards and Yahtzee, drank coffee, chatted and laughed.

My visit was extended by the weather, so I also got to catch up with old friends. Among them was a dear friend whom I met over 40 years ago. At that time, she was a Russian history scholar; today she's the victim of memory loss.

She still displays her marvelous humor when I recount happy events we once shared, and I realize it's the happy stories we carry forward; this is probably why my brother and other combat veterans never talked about their war experiences. They were trying to forget so that they could move forward with good lives that had been interrupted with horror.

Since I'm in the process of trying to gather my life story for my descendants, I decided that I didn't need to look in dusty files; we had already shared the stories, repetitively. They will pass from generation to generation until worn out.

It's the written records that were filed away because we didn't want to remember them yet. We embellish the stories that make us laugh and rarely refer to those that made us sad.

I went through every folder in six drawers of files over the weekend, partly to separate into what could be chapters in my life, and partly to discard trivia. The happy memories either confirmed or amended my stories, but the others documented some events that I had deliberately erased from my memory.

Some Wyoming legislators really said dreadful, nasty things about me, partly because they didn't like women they perceived to have power, and partly because I refused to pretend that what they were doing was either ethical or logical. I admit I wasn't what a gracious woman could and maybe should be.

One of the files held evidence that a few well-placed legislators tried to convince the University of Wyoming's Board of Trustees that they would lose some funding support if they hired me. The good news is that the university refused to be intimidated and did hire me. I'll never know whether it was a coincidence that they ran out of funds within six months. It doesn't matter because my next job at the University of Wisconsin was one of the most fruitful, happy and important ones I ever had, preparing teachers and principals with new knowledge and skills in math, reading and drama.

One of the characters in "Alice in Wonderland" said that "It's a poor sort of memory that only works backward" and I've found over a long life of good memories, it makes sense.

It's the happy memories we take forward that help us grow and approach life with hope, enthusiasm and anticipation. If we looked backward at the rough times, we'd be mired in quicksand that sucks us into despair.

Fortunately, I have "a grand memory for forgetting" (Robert Lewis Stevenson) and it's getting better all the time. And that means I don't have to write about my life because I've already told everybody who will listen the stories about the best parts.

I've given up on cleaning out the files, so my relatives can either throw it all out or sort through them for the rest of the story. I recommend holding the happy ones close to your heart.

Finish Something

It really is 2014 and I must say that I entered it reluctantly. Have you ever entered a new year wanting to shout, "Get back here, I haven't finished this year yet!"? It's true that you're also grateful that you're still here and another year has passed, but if you're over 65, do you really want to shout, "Hurrah, I'm another year older and if I'm careful I may live to be 90 or 100"?

You can see the problem: you may be grateful, but not exuberant, especially if you had in mind several things you wanted to accomplish just in case next year doesn't come. So between the weather (which made it mandatory that you stay in because it was too slippery to walk and ill-advised to drive), and the embarrassment of writing the same resolutions you had last year, your day was more morose than celebratory.

You have just one choice: you move on. But moving on doesn't mean "letting go" for those of us who must finish what we start. So, personally, I resolve to continue my lifelong efforts to support, promote and improve public education.

Admittedly, I've never finished any job I had. There were always things I still wanted to do. I wanted to help make the Wyoming Department of Education more efficient; I wanted to expand the understanding and activities of the Wyoming Humanities Council; I wanted to increase United Way's services to those in need. Recently, I wanted to build better ways to connect funds with school board goals by expanding the dialogue about distribution to schools to see whether that would improve accountability for learning.

As we move on in age and circumstance, we never really feel like we've finished something, and finishing seems even more important as you become more aware of the fragility of life. We're in more of a hurry than ever and at the same time, want to hold back Father Time. For those of us who are never satisfied with the progress being made, there's only one epitaph: "But I'm not done."

Unfortunately, in this country, state and community, there's the tendency for others to decide when you're done. It's called age bias or retirement and all you have to do is listen to those who are "aged" but conscious, energetic and active. They haven't given up, but the wise have moved on to pleasant pastimes. They dance, they visit, they travel, they volunteer for only those things that give them good company and a casual, life-sustaining cause.

But some of us aren't ready because if we've spent a lifetime in education, the drop-out rate and the quality of what has been taught haunts us. We know that youngsters can find ways to recapture the academic things they missed, but they'll never recapture the social experiences that nurtured the foundations they needed to transition from child to adult. Parents and other adults are aware that quitting school is like diving off the dock into murky, deep water without a life jacket or goggles.

But the student doesn't know it until they've struggled to survive and realize that it now may take several years or a lifetime to get to the point that three years of high school might have brought them.

Is it possible to "move on" when we have over 40 years of knowledge and experience that could help find some answers? There aren't many opportunities or places left to finish what we started. This is the time and this is the place.

Does it make sense to work together to tackle an important issue before we move on? I think so and I'm taking advice from the musical "Seven Brides for Seven Brothers": "I ain't done 'til I say I'm done," and that means I'm not moving on until I've done everything I can for public education. I'm just trying a new format ... if we aren't successful in making public policy, let's try influencing it, together.

My Favorite Things

Some days it seems as though I don't like anything that's happening around me. The world seems off-kilter, and I'm out of sorts.

At least that's what a good friend who stopped by for coffee indicated last week when she asked if anything made me happy. I admit that being a senior seems to trigger an unenthusiastic critical streak bordering on cynicism, but that's not the real me. We seniors only seem like cynics because we're really incurable optimists who have finally faced reality.

Just to prove it, I'm writing about some of the things that make me happy. I encourage you to sing "These Are a Few of My Favorite Things" because singing helps both our mood and our memory.

Near the top of my list of happy things are hand-written letters and thank-you notes. I don't like emails; mine are usually misunderstood and yours are cold. A written note is ever so much better than a verbal one. Besides, you can keep it in your collection of stuff. Handwritten messages that come in the mail tell us a lot about people by the way they phrase a sentiment, the quality of the paper, the handwriting, the smell from the perfume, pizza or dusty purse, and the date on the envelope. Emails or texts don't tell you these things; their message is they're in a hurry and use abbreviations because they have little or no regard for the English language.

I find that a dining table dressed with silver and stemware, grandmother's dishes, candles and cloth napkins gives me a warm aesthetic high. While it's no pleasure putting things away when you can't remember which cupboard they came from, there's something elegant about a nicely set table. A hand-made runner by your favorite quilter, a bowl of poinsettias and name cards make us feel connected to family traditions and sentimental values. It stimulates our desire to watch old movies with Jimmy Stewart and Margaret O'Brien.

I love it when people dress up to attend a symphony, opera, wedding or funeral. It just doesn't seem appropriate to wear shorts, sweatpants or torn jeans, cut off at the knees, and blouses cut down to your navel at such events. The first opera I ever attended I wore a formal gown and dined at an outdoor restaurant in D.C. to hear Sutherland and Pavarotti in "Lucia de Lammermore." At least I think it was Sutherland and Pavarotti, but maybe I'm thinking of the record.

Speaking of records, in spite of having a Bose radio/CD, I still like to play records on a turntable. I enjoy the scratches and other sounds; they remind me of other times, places and people. An imperfection in music, unless someone sings off-key, makes you feel like you're in the concert hall, coughs and all.

It feels good when service people and children call me Mrs. or even Ms. And it's especially heart-warming when children do. Sometimes I long for the working days when staff actually addressed me as Doctor or Professor. I'm ashamed of myself to admit this because my parents taught us to always be modest and the title "doctor" seems like bragging unless you're a medical person. I'm heartened and startled to meet young people who are talented but self-effacing, because they're rare. That's probably because we're now telling all children they're "winners" whether they've exhibited any talent or made any effort at all.

The world seems more civil when people talk to each other in complete sentences. I especially enjoy it when they don't agree with each other, but then, I believe in constructive conflict and loyal opposition. I realize that some people have never heard of those civil ideas.

I like TV dramas without background music, movies with implied violence or sex, and speech that articulates words. I don't care how accurate a weatherman is if his voice sounds like rain falling on a tin roof.

I like Sunday morning talks with my daughter and late evening talks with sons, watching the antics of a squirrel on my deck, having coffee with friends, book club discussions and reading lots of books.

I especially like walks anywhere with young children. They see things differently and, often, more accurately than adults. As my then-four-year-old grandson said during a walk on the mountain, "If I let go of your hand, Gramma, you'll roll down the hill like an Indian rubber ball."

You can stop singing and humming now. It's the little things that make us cheerful, and the big things we deplore. Even Mary Poppins couldn't make the current world medicine go down with a spoonful of sugar.

Random Thoughts

An essay is supposed to be about an issue, with a topic, arguments for and against, and a conclusion.

I thought of several topics and couldn't quite develop them this week, so let's call this a column of random thoughts.

The first occurred to me in the shower. I know I'm supposed to be saving water, but I love hot water on my neck and shoulders; my neck and shoulders aren't dirty enough to justify five full minutes of washing, but I indulge myself. I do turn off the water in the kitchen sink, and try not to run it over the lawn and onto the sidewalk.

Thinking about water reminds me that I lived in a small town and that 10- to 14-year-olds had to carry water from the town pump. This wasn't so bad in the winter since I had a sled for the five-gallon milk can, but it certainly developed muscles during the summer. We had to be careful with water, and it always perplexed me, since I was the one assigned to tote it, that Mother scrubbed the floors much too often so that we could eat off them, or so she said. "My floors are so clean you could eat off them," she said, so I did ... just once. She didn't think it was funny at all when I left the table and dumped the food off my plate onto the floor.

As extravagant as she was with water for the floors, she saved her and my sister's bath water for me in order to get the full use out of it. That's because I lived a more active life than anyone else; I played softball and other games that got me dirty. I was more patriotic than my sister because I waded into swamps and garbage trying to find scrap metal for the war effort, and I had a whole book of victory stamps I purchased towards the war, and she didn't.

I realize now that the trips to the river during the summer weren't for recreation, but for bathing. In retrospect, an added benefit was that my father placed us on a log and then rolled the log so we ended up scuba diving without air tanks. My sister cried a lot, and that annoyed Dad, and that meant he praised me for being brave, so maybe it was recreational after all.

It seemed to me that it didn't take much to send my sister into a flood of tears. As an adult, she acquired an iron fist in a velvet glove, but thinking of her made me contemplate another issue that may become an essay some day. What, I asked myself, made people needy? Was it because they wanted to be needed and felt that nobody needed them? Is the human race divided into two kinds of people: those who need and those who want to be needed? Is there a third category of those who neither need/want anything, and aren't willing to help/give anything?

Do needy people become entitled, i.e., believe they deserve because they're worthy, or because they're victims?

Is it false advertising to imply that half-and-half has equal parts of cream and milk? Why is it called condensed milk when it isn't? How come I can't find any blue shoe polish? All blue shoes can't be suede, can they? If we restore the right of law-abiding citizens to carry weapons into government buildings, are non-law abiding citizens also allowed to do so? Is it possible to be a patriot without carrying a concealed weapon? Is it possible to be a good citizen by just flying a larger flag than your neighbor?

I wonder if any random thought can actually be developed into an essay, letter to the editor, petition to legislators, or a handbook for respecting other's space.

Spilling the Bucket

One of the fads nowadays seems to be making bucket lists; even younger people seem to be doing it. That's a list of the things you want to do, be or have before you kick the bucket. That, of course, is a euphemism for leaving for good, meeting your maker, going to the great beyond, dying.

I wondered where the expression came from, and found that its roots were uncertain. It could be from the word "buquet," referring to the beam on which pigs were suspended by their heels for slaughter; it could refer to the bucket the person stands on that has to be kicked away when being hung; or it could be the bucket used to collect for the widow who received a kick rather than a coin in her alms bucket.

All of those definitions could describe how we feel about leaving this world. In any case, I thought it might be good to think about what we want to put in the bucket before it's kicked, ignored or spilled. So I decided to make a list that isn't likely to be kicked but, hopefully, will just be slightly tipped to dribble a little.

I've started it in anticipation of my 85th birthday, which I suddenly realized means I'm "getting on." Even though I feel great, it's wise to fill my bucket right now lest someone kicks my empty bucket. Besides, I always try to remind family and friends way ahead of time that I'm having a birthday so that I get funny cards and something for my bucket. It also occurred to me that if there were things I wanted to do, acquire or say, I better do so while I still have the energy.

A list isn't realistic if one's longings have already seeped out of a hole in the bucket. I love skating, but it requires quite a bit of balance, so I may place it in 10th place on my list. Mind you, I know the difference between ice on the rink and ice on the sidewalk — the experience is entirely different and the expectations aren't similar. Walking on ice is a bit like trying to place your legs in your trousers in the middle of the room and taking a header, whereas skating is gliding across an arena until you hit the sideboards.

At the top of the bucket list will be my desire to become an opera diva. Probably that opportunity has passed, but it's still possible to imagine I sound really good in the shower. My dog, Rowdy, also appreciates opera and often is heard accompanying me.

Second on the list is a driving trip to northern California to see Son #3 and family, or to Lake Superior to see son #1 and family, including a three-year-old great grandson, and to Canada to visit my sister. Last year, my daughter convinced me that I shouldn't drive that far by myself. She said I risked falling asleep. I should think I would have proven myself by traveling the Medicine Bow highway twice during the holiday storms. But she contended that even I'm not likely to fall asleep in a ground blizzard or on ice-packed roads. She worries about boring freeways, but believes that if I take rural roads, she won't be able to find me if "something" happens. I'm going anyway.

A few years ago, I took a paddle boat trip down the Mississippi, and I'm adding a trip down the Rhine or some other European river to my list. Indeed, I intend to move it to the top of the list if I win the lottery or a wealthy stranger lends me funds I can pay back over the next 10 years.

I'm going to put the desire for more great-grandchildren on the list, but I suppose that because of my insistence that my grandchildren marry first and give birth second, it probably won't happen.

It may not be appropriate to place objects you want on the list, but I think it's time I have a lawnmower with a starter button. Pulling the cord really jerks my arm out of the socket, and when that happens I use disgusting words like "h---," and that doesn't reflect either the maturity and dignity I try to project, or where I hope the journey takes me.

Besides, it's hard to pat oneself on the back for being independent when the arm is limp.

I'd like to swish around the dance floor one more time, and that might require a new flowing evening dress and high heels, and music other than a polka, but it's important enough to put somewhere on the list.

Just once, I'd like to buy a first edition book for $2 and sell it for $500 rather than the other way around. While I'm at it, I'd like a bucket of books. They don't seep easily.

Who started this silly notion of making a bucket list anyway? Maybe we'd be smarter if we emptied the buckets of things we shouldn't have done rather than fill it with things we still want to do, be or have. Truth is, we don't kick the bucket anyway; we usually bump it so it spills drop by drop.

Thanks, But No Cooking

As grandmothers have become older and are supplanted as the holiday cooks for forgetting to turn on the oven or other techniques, they're invited to the join their offspring or go to a hotel buffet with other oldsters.

The fact is that most of us who have reached the stage of not wanting to cook would rather look at holidays as the days we gather memories, not food. We would rather not watch football games or send the children outside or to a different room to play. We'd rather do something that makes memories as a family or just think of Thanksgivings past.

Thanksgiving was set aside to count our blessings, and most of us point to our families as our biggest blessings, in a relaxed setting that revives memories and elicits lots of laughter. One of my favorite Thanksgivings was at our cabin in the Medicine Bow National Forest west of Laramie in below zero temperatures.

As a native of International Falls, Minn., I was accustomed to bitter cold. Below-zero temperatures, underwear rolled up and stockings rolled down, was an opportunity to show our toughness and demonstrate that the freezing temperatures didn't cause varicose veins. Cold, I told the children, was invigorating. Wrapped so they could barely move, they agreed.

The cabin could sleep 10, providing we were all family and doubled up. And so we settled in, close and warm.

The fire in the woodstove was turning it amber, and my daughter-in-laws thought building a fire in the antique Monarch cook stove would complete the picture of the early Thanksgivings. A little skeptical because I felt fortunate to have electricity and an electric range and viewed the cook stove as a conversation piece, but I agreed. Since it wouldn't hurt to have another source of heat, the men split wood in kitchen stove size, and added a dangerous addition to the staging of our pioneer drama.

After a couple of hours we recollected the truth that it took a lot of talent to regulate the temperature to bake something in a cook stove, and turned on the electric oven, adding that to our list of things for which to be thankful during the blessing.

Since we still had time for outdoor activities, the four grandchildren and I decided to skate and sled on the beaver ponds, from which we were getting water that had to be boiled to prevent giardia. It was frozen solid, and we had a wonderful time even though once flopped on the sled, the bulky winter clothing made it hard to get up.

Sons and daughters stayed in the cabin, even though I had taught them to do things with their kids. I felt the cold first, and gathered the children back to the cabin after what seemed like hours, but was only long enough to get out of helping with the dishes. Did I mention that washing dishes at the cabin was a big job because we carried our water and had to heat it?

By the time the dishes were done, it was time to eat snacks and play Pictionary or Yahtzee. No one would play Rummy with me anymore since there was a rumor that I cheated to win every time. So dice games seemed more reliable or at least fair. The male grandsons preferred Battleship until they realized strategy rather than raw force was involved.

The first contest was over who would get the two best artists in the family. It was against the rules to have best artists on one team, so the two best were always the favored captains. It has always seemed to me that one knows nothing about winning Pictionary until challenged with a card that simply says "skipping."

The evening ended with the eldest son's (the artist and museum director) team winning as usual. I thought, being the mother, I would get my choice of children to sleep with since my blood was thinner than anyone else's. But, no, the family decided one more game would decide who could choose children. Confident I would win Trivial Pursuit, I agreed. Who knew there were complete games about 1960s culture?

I slept with three sleeping bags and the dog, and the kerosene lamps were supposed to provide additional warmth.

In spite of the cold, I was filled with gratitude: we had beaver ponds and milk cans; we had electricity and kerosene lamps; we had laughter, happy children, warm beds, and comforts waiting us back in town. We could dare to embark on pioneer adventures every now and then.

Though the older folks are limited in skating, biking, hiking and digging for dinosaur bones in 2011, we will fill ourselves with joy over this Thanksgiving and those past, and give thanks.

Abstract or Practical

When I graduated from college with a major in both English and History, my mother had tears in her eyes when she said, "That's nice honey, but what can you do?"

For many at that time, and even today, the humanities were viewed as esoteric trivia completely unrelated to life. Thank goodness there were those in Congress in 1970 who wondered whether there should be a balance between the new commitment to science (because of Sputnik) and those who thought that art and the humanities had something to do with the nation we'd become.

Nevertheless, within a year, when they launched the state-based programs, they took a practical route: we were to focus the humanities on public policy issues. The idea wasn't to just support academic humanists in their normal scholarly activities or in teaching college kids, but to figure out how to get adults to utilize the humanities.

What an opportunity to connect our interest in public policy and literature, philosophy and history! But I can tell you it was harder than it appeared. One of our early efforts I shall never forget. It was a stretch to connect literature to the development of a water/sewer system in Rock Springs and quite another to send out a philosopher. But we did. We told him to sit in an open air meeting and answer questions.

Well, in those early years we may not have shed a lot of light on either the humanities or public policy, but within a year we knew the value of the experiment ... getting the academic humanists off the campus to contemplate and demonstrate why their disciplines did have something to do with the decisions made in a community, state or nation.

The point was, we realized that it wasn't just the information contained in literature or history, but the process of contemplating what it meant to be human, to untangle dilemmas, to solve problems. These were the disciplines that described human actions, motivations, mistakes and victories.

One of the first controversies we encountered was a project of viewing and discussing horror films. Some people thought it was a horrible waste of public funds, but it was a prime example of some of the values that needed to be discussed and applied to our behaviors. Bram Stoker may not have elicited the same respect as Shakespeare, but in many ways, the depiction of Frankenstein may have been as significant as the fatal flaws of Othello.

The original purpose of the humanities may have been to prepare a few young men (the potential leaders, the elite) to be effective speakers and have secular virtues, in other words a preparation for the life a few would live to guide the many.

In those first years, we didn't apply for state funds, perhaps because we wanted to see what a public program guided by a volunteer board could accomplish. Maybe it was because we knew that it was an experiment, and that mistakes would be made and that the program would have to be nurtured and grown. We were building a different relationship with the public where learners weren't a captive group judged by the instructors, but a volunteer group that may very well question the instructor.

My doctoral study found that the participants in the early humanities program were educated, more female than male, highly involved in their communities and between the ages of 40 and 60.

In a long career in education at the local, state and national levels, this was and remains my favorite of all jobs. We worked with a variety of people who were serious about what it takes to be good citizens, what these studies contributed to problem-solving, creativity and independent thinking, and what it means to be human over all time, places, circumstances and cultures.

But one of the reasons I'm still enthusiastic about the public humanities programs is that I'm so pleased and proud with how it has evolved, changed and become even more relevant to preserving the capability of civil discourse about public issues so important to our survival. The Wyoming Humanities program has grown from the puny foundation we laid 45 years ago to provide important discussions in a civil manner about Wyoming issues.

Under Penalty of Law

Have you ever noticed that practically everything has a warning on it, as though we haven't an ounce of common sense? For example, do we need a warning to "unwrap before cooking"?

Worst of all are the prescription medications that have pages of deleterious results worse than the malady they're supposed to treat.

I hesitate to take a medication for high blood pressure when the three-page warning indicates that if I have any other problems such as heart disease, kidney failure, low sodium or potassium levels, have been stung by a bee, swelling of the hands, face, lips, eyes, throat or tongue, difficulty in breathing, swallowing or hoarseness, having surgery or taking anesthesia, I should tell my doctor before taking the blood pressure medicine. Does this mean "ever" or "anticipated" or right now? I was stung by a bee once.

I'm so inhibited by the warnings that I still have a 50-year-old mattress that I keep in the garage because I'm afraid to discard the tag "under penalty of law." No one else can use it, and neither can I, but what happens if the tag is removed by critters in the dump and the authorities in charge of warnings find out it's mine?

Even if the pill we were taking lands on the floor in the cat hair, we're not supposed to flush it or throw it in the garbage, but take it to the police station or hospital. But what's the penalty for distributing dirty pills, especially at a police station?

Television ads are especially frightening. You're urged to take a medication for depression that may cause you to commit suicide. That seems like a really high-risk solution to what could be a well-intentioned remedy to life's "downers." Personally, I'd rather turn on "Madame Butterfly," have a good cry and drink a cup of tea than risk the possible side affects of an anti-depressant.

Does it make sense that older adults who usually need more medications than young adults have the longest list of medications that are "inappropriate"? Thank goodness we don't know what most of them are. What's meprobamate, flurazepam, chlorpropamide or dicyclomine? We may have been taking them for years and become immune, so why give us a list now when we don't care if we ingest something that's not good for us?

Even if we look at the side effects, we can't tell if we've taken something we shouldn't. If I'm clumsy, unsteady, drowsy or dizzy, it could be the result of falling off the first rung of the step stool, and not some drug I unknowingly swallowed.

Some pills cause memory impairment and confusion and that could be a normal condition on Monday, not the result of flurazepam in the wine. Blurred vision may simply be the result of not cleaning our glasses, and not some terrible disease we can't pronounce.

If you've ever had a cat or dog that sneaks onto the bed after you fall asleep, you need not worry that a dry mouth and confusion are caused by belladonna alkaloids, and simply conclude that cat and/or dog hair could cause dry mouth.

There are many warnings. Don't spray the apple trees, just eat the worms. Don't let kids talk to strangers, but let them cruise the internet unsupervised. Don't put wrapped food in the oven, unless the oven is off, or never. Put side A to side B and then hook it into C, and if that doesn't work, put the extra pieces in the junk drawer.

We need to be selective about which warnings we take seriously, and which ones we don't. Personally, I believe the way we get around medication warnings is to stop taking meds and substitute a daily glass of wine. I agree not to spray the apple trees, but refuse to follow directions about how to put pre-cut furniture together.

However, it seems to be a good idea to never, ever take the tag off a mattress. It may be attached to the springs or the baffles and go flat before you've shaped it to your body, or removing it could get you arrested by the trash collectors.

The Wyoming Way

Have you ever wondered why the smallest things can send you off into a stuttering, muttering grouch, while a crisis met and resolved makes you into an invigorated, joyful, expansive, forgiving optimist?

Why does a baby's response to a clicking tongue make us want to hum "Climb Every Mountain" the rest of the day, while a person who pushes his cart against our ankles in the grocery checkout line sends us into a paroxysm about the human condition?

Is this Othello's fatal flaw? Is this Hawthorne's dark veil? Is this the Code of the West? Is the Wyoming Way drifting into another state, leaving us acting like the "feds," whoever they are?

What's happening to the Code? Was it reflective of the rural culture? Can we rely on babies and beautiful sunsets and generous help from strangers and neighbors to confirm that we still live by the Code? And if it seems as though the Code is violated regularly, can we simply blame those outsiders who came here to get jobs or stay on when the bust comes?

Are those non-Wyomingites the ones who abuse and neglect children, rob convenience stores, get in gun fights, run people over, and drink, smoke and carouse? Does the Code address racial, gender and age discrimination?

The point is, it only takes a bash in the ankles by a grocery cart to make you wonder what's happening to the Wyoming Way. The Code of the West means something when endorsed by the Natrona County School District, business community and the Boys and Girls Clubs. It can't be violated lightly, and it's time we thought about it.

Code 1: "Live each day with courage" means we should speak up if we see injustice, prejudice and dishonesty, and remember that female courage isn't aggressiveness, but courage.

Code 2: "Take pride in your work" means coming early, staying late and paying attention to details.

Code 3: "Always finish what you start," but that doesn't mean arguments, because that's nagging.

Code 4: "Do what has to be done," but take your time and get group approval, and never throw out anyone's dirty Stetson or soleless boots.

Code 5: "Be tough, but fair" probably pertains to men unless women are sorting cattle or killing chickens or raising children.

Code 6: "When you make a promise, keep it" seems to exempt marriage or truthful vows, but does include arguments with someone who cheated you in a poker game.

Code 7: "Ride for the brand' may mean being loyal to Levi and Remington, but it probably means being loyal to Wyoming, though it's questionable whether it includes all the other states known as the "feds."

Code 8: "Talk less and say more" seems like a great idea, but doesn't mean someone needs to listen.

Code 9: "Remember that some things aren't for sale" covers things like integrity, honesty, loyalty, but doesn't cover great-grandmother's sterling or votes.

Code 10: "Know where to draw the line" means you stand by your principles no matter what evidence indicates they're in error or that they contradict each other. It's possible to hold principles like freedom and responsibility, individual rights and the common good, and loving your neighbor as yourself. Individual principles, such as the right to be armed, sometimes seem to supersede my right to life, liberty and the pursuit of happiness.

The Code didn't seem to cover as much as one Bible admonition to "do unto others as you would have them do unto you." Maybe that's the only code we need. It's important, however, to read it carefully. It doesn't say to do unto others BEFORE they do unto you.

When I consider the careless cart pusher who invades my space at the grocery store, I should be grateful, because when Wyoming has over 97,000 miles of space, it means that when we go indoors, it's comforting to press up against other people ... it's a sign of intimacy and warmth. Maybe pushing against others is the Wyoming Way of equality and justice, independence and freedom. If we think of a little cart-bashing as part of the Wyoming Way, it brightens our day because then we understand that only in the land of the free is my space your space.

CHAPTER 5

And the Winner Is ...

One of the writers in my OLLI class wrote a hilarious piece about waiting in vain for the Publisher's Clearing House to arrive at her door to tell her she had won. As usual, this piece was funny because it was so true. First of all, one has to expect to win for a good reason: you deserve it.

That philosophy is so pervasive, we hardly question it anymore. Somewhere, sometime in the past 20 years or so, we began to confuse equity with equality. One means to be fair and impartial, and the other means being the same in all respects. I suppose it doesn't take a very big leap to conclude that we deserve whatever anyone else has, or that all children are champions.

We all love children, or think we do, and believe, perhaps, that each can become a champion if their unique "talent" is exposed and practiced, but excellence may require some effort. With all the faults we may find with too much emphasis on sports, we have to concede that at least they develop the connection between effort and outcome.

That must be hard for coaches and others to do, since the children have already had years of being rewarded for just being there. Whether this stemmed from Freud or some other person who thought he knew something about the human brain, I can't quite fix as a starting point, but there's no question about whether we collectively decided that little egos were so fragile, we must not indicate in any way that certain behaviors would be rewarded and other behaviors wouldn't. And so we have children running wild in church and in school, experimenting sexually before they're mature enough to do so, and demonstrating that with no effort at all, one can "succeed." Last week, I discovered that we older folks weren't just fantasizing about the past when I discovered a book entitled, "You Are Not Perfect" by a young teacher named David McCullough Jr. I had concluded that not teaching a child the route to self-discipline (through a demonstration of cause and consequence) is a terrible disservice to the child, but McCullough goes further. He says that the message to the child is that he's perfect and mustn't go so far outside the boundaries or he'll be in danger of being rejected because, after all, the parents must consider themselves perfect parents.

The mystery is how the parents expect the child to grow up to have that perfect job with a high salary when he'll probably be hired by an older person who believes that table manners are important, that respect for others is essential, or that relationships can't be built without considering another person's habits, beliefs and fears.

There are those who say that we're living in a child-hating society and, ironically, those who are pampered with permissiveness are causing the same damage as those who neglect with self-centeredness or busy-ness.

When our grandmothers asked, "What is the world coming to?", we just rolled our eyes in condescension. Now we're grandmothers and we're asking the same thing. How will our children survive without self-discipline, without concern for the other person, without a sense of community? Can they survive when the only communication is electronic and the only hugs they get are verbal from strangers on their "friends" list?

Why is it significant that on the only international test that American youth came out first in was self-assurance? Is it healthy to be proud of ourselves for no good reason at all? Perhaps there's a larger plan involved with the Pope's visit to the U.S. at this time. Is there only one person of major influence in the world who's humble? It certainly hasn't been demonstrated at the Bishop's level ... locally or nationally. Personally, I expect more from those who wear the accouterments of spirituality than I do of those who are clearly sinners, such as this one I know better than anyone else.

So what's the world coming to if we're all "special"? I suppose it's possible, but only if none of us think we are or act as though we are. As one of the presidential candidates has pointed out, if he's a winner, then the rest of us are losers, no matter what!

But What Can You Do?

Last week I participated in two momentous events: the 45th anniversary of the Wyoming Humanities Council and the marriage of one of my three granddaughters.

Like so many events in our lives, they were connected. The personal blended with the professional, the past became a part of the present. My granddaughter attended a liberal arts college (St. Olaf) and has a career based on her study of the humanities. On the day after the wedding, her father (my son) took his brother, sister, niece and me on a tour of Hamline University, the oldest university and liberal arts college in Minnesota, and from which he and I graduated.

The multi-colored fall leaves, the serenity garden, Old Main and the GI Quonset huts for married students that once stood where the new athletic training center now stands, all brought back memories of the four years I spent there making friends, learning and growing, courting, marrying and having my first child. I stood on the very spot my mother occupied when she congratulated me by saying, "That's nice, honey, but what can you do?" She didn't think that a B.A. with majors in English and history made me very employable, but then she didn't think that after marriage and a child I would be employed outside the home in any case. It was, after all, the 1950s.

Her words haunted and inspired me for the next 60 years that I spent in education and related fields. I responded then, and continue to contend, that a degree in the humanities prepares us for anything we want to do, and is essential to the quality of our lives. But I came to realize that the attitude in the 1940s and '50s still remained with many people in 1965, and even today, when the Wyoming state-based humanities program was launched.

Even though Congress, in creating the National Endowment for the Humanities in 1965, said they thought that American leadership was based as much on the achievement of ideas and the spirit as on superior power, wealth and technology, they instructed the state-based programs to use the humanities to explore "timely" issues.

Because there were still those who thought that studies of English, history, literature and philosophy were effete, intellectual trivia, the state-based Council decided in their second year to get more specific about "timely issues" and demonstrate that the humanities were valuable in discussing public policy issues, i.e., issues upon which collective decisions would be made.

From the beginning back to the studies in ancient Greece, the humanities had two camps: those who believed they were valuable for their own sake, and those who thought they should have some practical use.

Personally, I never doubted that what I learned about human nature in literature classes, other cultures in language classes, and the merging of public events that led to historical crises in history, was practical knowledge. Further, we were reminded that the purpose of education wasn't employment, but citizenship. Hamline University, founded by a Methodist bishop, emphasized public service on a daily basis.

Perhaps most of all, we learned that there was a connection between what was happening in history, what was being written in novels and short stories, what was contemplated in philosophy, and what the world events of the 1930s and '40s had to do with life today and in the future.

The study of the humanities demonstrated that the knowledge of different people, times and places was transferable to current issues that demanded not only understanding, but the skills to approach problems. Fareed Zakara, in a new book entitled "In Defense of a Liberal Education," identifies several skills intrinsic to the studies called the humanities that go beyond reading, analyzing and dissecting. He contends that only in writing and speaking can you really understand what you learned and what you think in order to pass on and test those ideas with others.

As the trend seems to be moving towards making education a preparation for specific work, it's even more important to listen to what employers are saying about the broad and more basic skills of thinking, problem-solving, analyzing, synthesizing, innovating and working with others. These broader skills and knowledge can be applied to any employment because all demand a problem-solving process that helps us come up with solutions that serve us separately and together. It was a concept once called the common good.

So Mother, if you're watching, and I know you are, the family has produced three generations that can answer your question: the humanities prepared us to do SOMETHING.

Clichés and Other Indiscretions

A cliché, according to the Oxford Dictionary, is a "phrase or idea that has been used so often that it's no longer interesting or effective." I'm surprised that such a prestigious reference doesn't mention the fact that the first time any phrase was used it was probably clever, descriptive and meaningful. Indeed, a cliché may be reflective of our lives that start out so bright and original and gradually wear out.

The point is, clichés are over-used, stale and meaningless, or were metaphorically stretched to begin with. One that really confounds me is prefacing remarks with "all things being equal." Why do we say that when all things aren't equal?

We probably use it because we know that what we're proposing can never be implemented because conditions never remain the same and one can't rely on hoping nothing else happens to alter the original plan. If we're really not referring to a math or science project, we should simply use it as a disclaimer before we present an idea like "milk never sours" or something similarly profound.

I suppose it's no surprise that we use the financial term "bottom line," but forget that it means profit or loss and is meaningless unless both positive and negative concepts are recognized and discussed. We make it sound like it's the only conclusion to whatever argument or idea we've presented.

Really annoying is the expression "catalyst for change." This suggests that someone (a substance) can increase the rate of reaction without it affecting the person who solicited the situation that caused a reaction. If you didn't follow that, nether did I, so why do we use the term? If we mean change agent, why don't we say so, or is that now a cliché too?

When we say "the buck stops here," do we mean we take responsibility? Then why use a phrase from card playing that means it's your deal or you can pass it on?

If we really want to date ourselves, we can use a cliché that has mold on it like "this is the greatest thing since sliced bread." That must have been a benchmark event, especially if it marked the first time they packaged it too.

How about "cut to the chase"? That's an old film expression meaning if all else fails to get the audience's attention, stop and play the chase scene. It has come to mean "we're busy so get to the point."

Why don't we just say "this is a different way of looking at things" rather than saying "this is a paradigm shift"? I suspect we borrow phrases from science since most of us don't understand science. What's to understand? The lights go on when you flick a switch!

We also borrow from math, which some of us don't understand very well even though we know how to count back change for a dollar when most people don't. Why do we use the word "parameter" when we probably mean "perimeter"? Are we setting boundaries to ideas or to the process we use in discussing them?

When we say there's an "elephant in the room," do we mean there's a controversial issue that needs to be discussed? If there's an elephant in the room, how is it possible to recognize it's there and proceed to ignore it?

I wish we wouldn't use the term "collateral damage" to mean unintended consequences, when the term seems to have been coined as a polite way of saying innocent people died but we didn't mean it to happen.

I'm tired about hearing something is "politically correct." Let's just admit that if it's political, it's probably not correct nowadays. Civility is a different matter.

"Downsizing" should have been limited to talk about cars, not life, and whoever really believes that "failure isn't an option"? That falls into the same category as the "un-examined life."

Most annoying of all is the cliché "60 is the new 80." I can assure you that if you've lived another 20 years, there's a big difference between 60 and 80, and not only is 60 not the new 80, the very notion is an insult to the tolerance it took for those who are 80 to survive an additional 20 years "forever poised between a cliché and an indiscretion"* and other tribulations (*Harold McMillen, former British P.M.).

Creating A World-Class Education System

In a recent study of high performing schools around the world, Amanda Ripley identified several characteristics that could be guiding principles for American schools.

But first, we have to give up some of our cherished beliefs and myths:
1. That if we expect too much of children, they'll lose their self-confidence and sense of identity;
2. That memorization of facts makes us smart;
3. That diversity means we must lower standards to accommodate special physical and mental issues;
4. That "rigor" exists without equity;
5. That learning isn't hard work.

In a first-class system, teachers are well-prepared and expected to know more about teaching and learning than parents and students. This means that universities must increase the qualifications for entering the field and the measures for success before graduating education students. It may also mean that spending, class size, the use of data and parent visitation in the evenings, rather than when a classroom is filled with students, is useless.

In a high-performing system, parents visit classrooms periodically and observe students for at least a half-hour. Are they paying attention? Are they interested in what they're doing? Are they helping each other? Do they notice the visitors or are they working on what they're supposed to be doing?

What are the students doing? Why are they doing what they're doing? Ask the students, not the teacher. Do the students ask questions if they don't understand? Do they participate in discussions?

Do the parents share their ideas about schools' strengths and weaknesses? Or do they simply complain about how their own child is treated or performing? Do the parents defend the child, right or wrong, or let them make mistakes and then help them with better habits of the mind? Do parents read to the children, discuss the news? Provide learning opportunities?

Are the high-tech toys provided to the students used as learning tools or a waste of time, or worse? Is high-performing technology used in the classroom by all the students and with deliberation by the teacher?

Does the principal select the teachers, or are the teachers pre-screened by a central office that doesn't know the culture of the school building? Does the principal watch the teachers teach and help them become even more effective by giving them feedback? Do the teachers participate in the selection of the principal?

How is success measured? Are higher-order thinking skills and problem-solving measured? Is there a school plan for improvement every semester based on student performance?

Is praise used in moderation, and is there a clear connection between act and consequence?

How do the teachers and principals, parents and students know when the work is "rigorous" enough? Is it possible that if the bar is raised for everyone, everyone reaches higher than if the bar is left in place, regardless of performance?

Finally and perhaps the most important question is, what do the state, district and school believe is the purpose of schooling? Why was it declared mandatory and free for everyone between the ages of five and 18? Was it because, to paraphrase Jefferson, it's impossible to be free if we're ignorant? Shouldn't we expect certain knowledge to be handed down from one generation to the next? Shouldn't graduates of public schools know about the formation of their own government and the principles upon which it was founded? Shouldn't we expect each generation to be exposed to our art, literature, language, history, and the history of western civilization upon which it was based?

Shouldn't the skills being taught in our schools be the skills that preserve a self-governing society (such as decision-making, communication, creativity, entrepreneurship, critical thinking) as well as how to do a job? The skills should be life skills, not simply employment skills unless they're one and the same.

In the international study, Ripley came to these conclusions:
1. Schooling in the U.S. was easier.
2. American parents structured their children's activities.
3. American parents place more importance on sports than international parents.
4. More emphasis is placed on praising students than in other countries.

In a book by nationally-known educator John Goodlad, he said that the study and practice of democracy in our schools has weakened. It has weakened because we no longer seem to believe that the primary purpose of education is for responsible democracy, i.e., self-government.

A major question is whether we've created a system with children at its center or a system that serves adults. All you have to do is look at the organization and structure of an individual school, district or state education system to answer that question. If it's designed to be convenient for, or to give power to, the adults, then it's probably not centered on students.

Did You Hear What I Heard?

While it's true that many of us aren't hearing as well as we once did, it's also possible that we can't believe what we're hearing. As we enter the Advent season, there are those who claim that if we greet others with "Happy Holidays," we dishonor Christianity. I always thought it was a way of showing respect for my Jewish and other friends who may not be celebrating the same event that I am.

There seem to be a lot of ways to misinterpret language or draw strange conclusions from it. I noticed a shopping advertisement that exhorted us to find the true meaning of Christmas under the tree. That seemed just so serious a breach of the meaning that I decided to explore other uses and misuses of language.

For example, I may have already told you about one son's version of the "Twas the Night Before Christmas" when he said that the father ran to the window to see what was the matter, and instead of throwing up the sash, he vomited the sash.

I still see a teenage son sitting on the kitchen counter, complaining that he didn't understand why, at our house, you could say what you wanted but you couldn't do what you wanted. I said I'd consider his thought on the matter, but in the meantime, he should remove his butt from the kitchen counter.

A few years ago, a couple of men named Cathcart and Klein wrote a book called "Aristotle and an Aardvark" to help us understand political and other double-speak. It took awhile to find it because I paused during my search to appreciate other books that I forgot were shelved.

Frankly, their guidance didn't help. We've almost adapted to double-speak, faulty conclusions, false analogies and people who lie by answering a different question than the one that was asked. Though trying to interpret the message, values or meaning of such speech that doesn't tell us anything and is annoying, the idea that we should manage to cut off what people say because there are "trigger warnings" is more repugnant to me.

That doesn't mean we should ignore the use of language to disguise rather than elucidate meanings, especially if the language is used to lead us astray. Honest mistakes are often amusing and sometimes even thought-provoking. A recent a newspaper article said that an action had been used to "bridge the gasp." Considering the subject, I realized that the added "s" wasn't a mistake at all, but an editorial comment.

It was tempting to take some examples out of the current political campaign, but I hesitate to point out the obvious and, besides, it would sound uncivil or like we're making fun of others.

So I'll give you some Cathcart examples. We could allude to Lizzy Borden as an expert in cutlery rather than an axe murderer. We could accept the idea that if schools won't be feeding children for 13 days, they will, therefore, be food insecure during that whole period, and that in spite of over 45 food banks in Casper, they'll starve. We could believe there's little difference between borrowing money without the lender's permission to feed our children and stealing.

We could conclude that pro-life is anti-abortion, that creationism is intelligent design but evolution isn't, or that terrorists are Muslims, therefore Muslims are terrorists. Or we could accept the notion that if someone says you're ugly, they really mean you're beautiful.

As Secretary Rumsfeld said many years ago, the absence of evidence doesn't mean there's evidence of the absence. Remember, he was talking about weapons of mass destruction. Not being a scientist, I don't know whether there has to be evidence of a void.

It does seem that in the absence of evidence, it helps to use the passive voice. Phrases such as "mistakes were made," "lies were told," "my homework disappeared," "lives were lost" explain what happened, but ignore why or how.

"Happy Holidays" may be double-speak after all. I say it to show respect for friends who don't celebrate the same event that I do, but it doesn't mean I'm not celebrating Christ's birthday. But couldn't "Happy Holidays" also honor the idea that others are saying Alleluia too?

History or Histrionics

One of the dilemmas in life is sorting out the difference between perception and paranoia, history and memory. In the first instance, if you think someone is out to get you and they are, you're perceptive. If they aren't, you're paranoid. In the second instance, which is what is on my mind today, if you're dealing with factual events that are documented, it's history. If you're writing about your life, you're counting on memory ... a rather selective, unreliable source.

I'm serving on the Alliance for Historic Wyoming and the Natrona County Historic Commission at the same time that I'm facilitating an OLLI writing class where several people are trying to compose their memoirs for their children and grandchildren.

As a historic preservationist, I want to save sites and buildings with historic significance that tell a story about past events and lifestyles. The Alliance spent two years compiling the data needed to nominate Dean Morgan Junior High as a historic site but are waiting for the NCSD to endorse/certify the application. It's an honor to have a building designated as a historic site, but some people believe that having a national designation for anything will destroy local control. In Wyoming, the tendency is to revere history more than politics, so the Alliance has high hopes.

The connection between my fascination with history and our tendency to want to record our lives is this: memory is very selective. We tend to deliberately forget the unpleasant, painful or embarrassing aspects of our lives, and remember the happy, constructive and productive times when we were the heroes. Sometimes we're more successful about resurrecting the painful if we can write it as fiction or poetry. Personally, I applaud dressing up poetry or fiction by drawing on our secret experiences, but deplore historians who attempt to do so by making up stories about historical events or figures. It does matter what we call it.

Is it possible for us to tell our stories without making ourselves look heroic? Probably not, unless we pretend it's someone else's story. Memory almost always places us center stage, and that's where the spotlight is. The negatives are there in the shadows, often forgotten for very good reason. We can't live happy lives by dragging along those heavy, negative experiences.

Yet we must inform ourselves of the events of the past in order not to repeat them. As someone said, "the past is prologue to the future." When we preserve schools or other buildings and sites, we're preserving both the positive and negative facts about a time period before us. The Wyoming School for the Deaf needs to be preserved, not because it's a beautiful building or because of happy memories, but because it served a unique purpose for children at a specific time in history.

In our writing class, we do preserve those moments that made us happy, proud or noble. And they're true because to us, they're important milestones and truths in our lives. But they're not histories. If we want history, someone else has to write it and if we're lucky, it's someone who either doesn't know us at all or likes us.

History considers the past as a whole, but slices out pieces that it connects with other pieces. Memoirs seem to slice off only the rind of our lives, leaving the core that's bruised or rotten uncovered. Samuel Pepys said that "memories are true and useful stars, while studied histories are stars joined in constellations according to the fancy of a poet," but I don't think so.

Perhaps it's a blessing that we remember how well we lived, laughed and loved, for then our memories can be a benediction, but it can never be called history. Those who limit themselves to facts must write history, but those of us intent on inspiring future generations need to write memoirs.

Just Follow the Proverbs

I thought about making some resolutions, but I've done that for about 65 years and haven't honored one. They included things like weight loss, cutting personal expenses, exercising, writing daily, reading five books a week, complimenting someone every day, calling my grandchildren more often, and disengaging from things that make me frustrated or depressed.

Resolutions are based on the idea that you can improve yourself, but I find that the "self" tends to either ignore or debate with you. I probably failed because denying your nature doesn't work, and most resolutions deny nature. That way, I'll know why I need to lose weight before adopting how to do so, and at the same time avoid resolutions I can't keep. It will be a better 2016 if we pay attention to the proverbs. As you know, proverbs are short, well-known truths or pieces of advice. We all appreciate advice and all we need to do is weave advice into action. It seems to me that it's far better to take pride in our principles than to defend our actions.

When I looked into using proverbial truths as guidelines for the new year, I found that the Oxford Dictionary lists 1,081 proverbs, plus all those listed in the Bible, "for acquiring a disciplined and prudent life."

For example, Proverbs 1:22 asks, "How long will the fools hate knowledge?" I like that one since I love knowledge and can justify being critical of those who don't, but I must admit that of the over 1,000 proverbs, I found more than half to be troublesome. I can't really subscribe to "better late than never" or "better safe than sorry," but I do think that to err is human, but to really foul things up requires a computer. I believe God forgives humans but no one should forgive computers.

It's probable that those who believe "if it ain't broke, don't fix it" probably never take any preventive action. It seems to me that it's a good idea to fix or improve something before it breaks. I dislike the idea that it's who you know rather than what you know that counts, probably because I spend more time reading than getting to know anybody who will help me get ahead. I'm reluctant to believe that ideas aren't more important to living a prudent life than forming calculated relationships.

Proverbs 15:1 says that "a gentle answer turns away wrath, but a harsh one stirs up anger"; I'm not sure that we shouldn't stir up a bit of discomfort from time to time.

If it's better to light a candle than to curse the darkness, we should probably keep our wits about us and offer a few solutions here and there. No doubt that charity should begin at home, but we must be cautious not to use it to cover a multitude of sins.

I've never thought the ends justify the means, but I think process counts, so I'm always quoting Robert's Rules of Order, formulating bylaws and designing systems. This isn't a popular notion, but I'm aware that fools rush in where angels fear to tread. I think it's a given that if at first we don't succeed, we try, try again … even into old age. Clearly, idleness is the root of all evil, but it's also true that the road to hell is paved with good intentions, so one has to be a bit selective about busy-ness.

I'm committed to the idea that a woman needs a man like a mermaid needs a bicycle, but that may be something we discover later in life. Some people believe there's no fool like an old fool, but my grandmother said that there's no fool like an educated fool at any age.

Sorting through proverbs helps a little, but they must be balanced. I suppose that sometimes what you don't know won't hurt you, but ignorance can't be bliss. If it weren't for hope, our hearts would break. The reader must sort and select among the thousands of proverbs to live by since, personally, I believe that brevity is the soul of wit and that the pen is mightier than the sword or the spoken word. But I don't resolve to prove it!

Poverty and Learning

Well, I was downsizing again last week, collecting books I could give to the library, when I ran across Hubert Humphrey's 1964 book, "War on Poverty." Needing a break from the psychologically exhausting work of downsizing, I decided to have a cup of coffee and read.

That triggered a desire to find out more about this 50-year war, so I dug into what poverty had to do with both the quality and quantity of results in our schools, and especially what impact it had on instruction here in Natrona County where over 38 percent of the children receive free or reduced lunches.

It dawned on me that I had a superficial idea that poverty was simply the lack of basic needs like food, clothing, shelter and the means of acquiring them. Lots of agencies are trying to solve the problem of hunger by distributing food every day to needy families, by providing free or reduced lunches, or making necessities available for entire families.

But after reading, thinking and mulling (which are fine substitutes for sorting and clearing), I realized that poverty is more than the lack of food, shelter and clothing, but "the extreme to which an individual does without resources such as financial, emotional, mental, spiritual, physical" (Payne). Furthermore, I concluded that it's the school that's the major, or perhaps the only, agency that attempts to provide the support system, relations, role models and the knowledge of the values the poor hold that prevent them from climbing out of poverty.

That's a huge function and one that exceeds by far the role of the teacher and function of the school of even 20 years ago. And it makes the school the real bastion of the war on poverty that's still with us in a county where almost half its students are receiving free and reduced lunches.

I realize that the situational poor will climb out of it with their middle-class values fairly intact, but the generational poor are mired in poverty, partly or mostly because their values are huge stumbling blocks to climbing out.

What does it mean to educate children who are from families who have lived in poverty for two or more generations? Are the values that most of us live by a mystery to the poor and are their values spreading into the middle-class?

Education seems to be the cure, but how difficult is it to teach children who feel inferior and powerless, are ashamed, humiliated, fearful, socially isolated, depressed, voiceless, with a different and limited language and cognitive process, disrespecting and distrusting, often developmentally delayed, neglected or abused? According to studies conducted by Ruby Payne and others, these are some of the characteristics of the generational poor.

Grouped together in the classroom, the teachers are expected to impart subject matter so that the children in poverty score well on standard tests. But first, the teacher must understand the culture students bring and how to instill the culture and values they need to learn, achieve and succeed.

It's been 50 years since we began the war on poverty, and it seems like the only thing that hasn't changed is the role expected of schools and teachers. It's they who have had to adapt both their expectations of what children know when they come to them at four or five, and how to adapt their instructional methods to serve the needs of the poor in a classroom that also has students that range from the disabled to gifted.

When legislators, parents and communities expect a better relationship between student results and funds spent, they're asking an economic question. But it's not about the relationship between money and student learning, it's about money and poverty. In neither case does money solve the problem.

What happens if poverty is about values, and the adoption of those values by the general population increases? Doesn't the war on poverty become a war on preserving the middle-class values and eradicating the values of distrust, dishonesty, lack of faith in the future, destiny rather than choice, despair rather than hope?

Most of all, shouldn't we recognize teachers as the warriors who are fighting to hold the line on the results of poverty? Shouldn't we recognize them as heroes who not only impart knowledge, but build the capacity to learn?

There's poverty right here in River City ... oh, sorry, in Casper. I just saw a good example of the terrific job teachers are doing when they expect the best. Thank you, Kelly Walsh teachers (especially Mr Stedillie), students and parents for overcoming the obstacles of cultural poverty.

Say What???

For those of us who grew up on "The Elements of Style," the changes in our language are almost too much to tolerate. But then I remembered that the American language has always been an annoyance, especially to the British, as early as the colonial days. If you like reading reference books, you may wish to re-read H.L. Menchen's "The American Language." It's very interesting, especially if you have the Casper cold or flu, which hangs on.

Language really is pretty fluid; it not only changes with new information and things we have to name, but with changes in the so-called culture. There are some descriptive new words, I suppose, but it seems to me we should draw the line at turning words into abbreviations. At the top of the list is "OMG." In my opinion, that's a much too informal way to be addressing our Creator.

And then there's "TMI" (too much information). Usually those who use it haven't half enough valid information and ought to label it gossip or libel. I'm not fond of SMH (shaking my head) either. Is there anything more exasperating than a teen that simply shakes his head at you? Haven't we taught them to spit it out and listen to reason, just like adults do?

BRB (be right back) ought to be outlawed. The trouble with human relationships is the tendency to multi-task, i.e., text to more than one person at the same time, and BRB isn't an appropriate apology. It's true that we're accustomed to first names instead of Mr. or Mrs., but I see no reason to be addressed as "u" followed by "r." Maybe there was no abbreviation for the incorrect singular "uzz."

Some people think that electronic media has ruined the English language, and it has certainly added to the demise, but we manage to mangle the language in other ways, and when the language is corrupted, so is the meaning.

My latest quarrel is with the word "innovative" as used to claim that rules, including Robert's, are unnecessary and that any attempt to conduct life in an orderly manner is simply outmoded. It seems that the definition of innovative is simply viewed as anything new, when some of us believe that something isn't innovative unless it's based on different, creative and unusual ideas or methods. If "innovation" is based on, or results in, chaos, it's not innovative, it's simply out of order or anarchy.

In other columns, we've mentioned the new meaning given to transparency, meaning you can see through; accountability, indicating responsibility; collegial to pretend we're equal; "give it up" for applause; and collaboration for getting other people to go along with what you've already decided. These words are the new vocabulary for power because we need to disguise our lust for it.

There are so many things that would improve by turning the clock back, so I decided to conduct serious research about what old phrases we should revive. If the language is going to change anyway, why not change it back to what it was when our ancestors were testing the limits of their independence from the "old" country, i.e., England?

How about resurrecting "whanger" to mean a noisy talker who makes use of political cant to amuse the rabble?

I liked my grandmother's invitation to "set a spell." It meant a short-term rest while we rocked. We need to slow people down, and if we put "set a spell" on our bumper stickers, people might actually stop when the light is red or even yellow.

I love the word "snicker" (and the candy too). I think we all ought to make fun of ourselves, raucously and wantonly, at the myths flowing over the internet. It adds a lot to civil discourse if we call our sarcastic reflections and petty disputes "squits" again; that's what the Puritans called it. The minister could implore us not to "squit" on our fellow parishioners.

When I first arrived in Casper in 1961, a well-known civic leader called me a "whipper-snapper." Now that I'm not 30 anymore, I understand why she was offended with the idea of some young person suggesting that zoning would be a good idea. In my defense, other young women who were taught to stay home with their children were flattered to be considered whipper-snapper housewives, even if it implied we were taking unwanted action.

There are other words that we should revive. Personally, I think if I were short and overweight, I would rather be called "squaddy" than short and overweight. If something is really special, even splendid, I think "splendiferous" is appropriate.

I deplore "tit for tat," which once meant if you kill my dog, I'll kill your cat. It's too bad "I'll treat you the way you treat me" has replaced

"I shall treat you as I would like to be treated."

I suppose there's a limit to how far back and how far forward we should go, since language is supposed to express ideas! Out here in the west we have a right to "wabble" about it.

Gadgets, Widgets and Wonders

Since gadget is defined as "a small mechanical device or tool," I suppose I can't count televisions, washing machines, computers, disc players, phones, car heaters and sprinkler systems as gadgets. But large or small, mechanical devices are ruining my daily peace of mind and self-concept. I realize that my friends and I learned things many years ago and have trouble adjusting, but are these changes really necessary?

No longer do we have an on/off switch for most devices. No, we have to push four buttons to turn on the TV. The pushing must be done in order and you must never touch the other buttons — ranging from A to D, Demand to DVR and Exit to Last — or you won't be able to see Jeopardy for a month. The buttons should have been clear about their functions so that I realized they had nothing to do with actually turning the TV on.

There are three circles of buttons in my almost-new car that turn on the heat or air conditioning. I turned on the heat by accident and it blew on me for several days after the temperature outside was over 70 degrees. I lived with it by opening the sunroof, which I discovered also by accident and then couldn't close. Fortunately I have a garage for rainy days.

The real challenge was turning on the sprinkler system. My daughter said it's simple, but she wasn't here to read the directions. First it says to set the time of day and then the date, but one hesitates because it may be tomorrow before you've figured out how to set the time and date, when you want it to water and how long you want it to run. The directions say nothing at all about how to dig up sprinkler heads that the dog has buried, nor how you direct the sprinkler heads to spray the lawn rather than the sidewalk.

As for computers, you have to adopt the neighbor's four-year-old to figure out how to pay your bills online, increase the type size on your manuscript, make columns, get rid of italics that appeared out of nowhere, and stop getting messages from strangers on Facebook. I was the one who set up computer training workshops for employees years ago, but never had to take the training to keep my job. That took an academic humanist with a knowledge of fatal flaws, creativity and ambition.

I do have devices I appreciate, such as my shredder. There's one switch which moves forward to grind up paper, and backwards to regurgitate it. I don't know why one would want to send the strips of paper back up again, but it's nice to have two choices even when only one makes sense.

I also appreciate my Bose Wave radio/CD. I manage to play music all the time and I can usually find public radio. It also has an alarm clock, but I have no need for the alarm clock so I haven't kept myself awake worrying about how it works. It faithfully dials to a station at 5 a.m. without fail.

My washing machine and dryer are fairly simple; I choose whites or colored, heavy or light, and leave it alone. It certainly beats the old washboard and wringer, but then I didn't get the fancy model that does other things that have something to do with getting clothes clean or bright or something.

Maybe it's just me and not the complicated electronics. I recall that after sewing three little pinafore dresses for a little girl (after having three sons), I gave up sewing because I couldn't understand the directions that seemed to tell me to put the woof to the weave, the back to the front, and sew everything inside out.

I can usually put bookshelves together since I've had quite a bit of experience and don't believe books should be piled vertically on the floor. There are usually directions that say attach A to B and B to C. Even here, however, one has to recognize that there's an inside and outside, and an upside and a downside to the construction, but this terminology is something I've seen before in literature.

It makes a difference whether we view things we're supposed to be able to operate as gadgets or devices. I prefer "devices" because of the multiple meanings. A device, according to the illustrated Oxford Dictionary (the best) is "a thing made for a particular purpose." That's enlightening, but isn't it important to understand the purpose? A secondary definition says a device is "an explosive contrivance." I certainly react that way. A less-used meaning of device is "a plan, scheme or trick." That's what I've said all along.

Even when we read the directions as a last resort, a person is left to their own devices. We can call a help line and try to understand the person with great expertise speaking Farsi or some other language.

I know many of us who need help can't hear directions in our own language and so we're left to our own devices.

Personally, I had this flash of insight: why not borrow a smart phone? It does everything: taking pictures to word processing, browsing the internet to sending emails. The trouble is, someone has to tell it what to do. Maybe robots ... but they're probably not gadgets or devices, but wonders.

Silence Is Not Always A Virtue

It occurred to me while doing physical labor that some of the virtues we were taught just don't seem to be true anymore. For example, a stitch in time saves nine? You'd have to be a quilter for that to apply to anything because it sure doesn't apply metaphorically to surgery.

How about "nothing ventured, nothing gained"? Lately it seems likely "if you venture, you will lose." The stock market must have been more predictable when someone said that.

How about "silence is golden"? Today's proverb seems to be "never apologize, never explain." Proverbs, as you know, are supposed to be one man's wit and all men's wisdom, according to Lord Russell who probably wrote advice for the common man.

I found several situations where silence is golden seemed an unlikely truth. Silence is not only worthless in a group trying to make a decision, it conjures several doubts about the trustworthiness of the individual. When a group needs an exchange of ideas but an individual withholds his voice until after the decision is made, is it arrogance, especially if it's preceded by "I tried to be quiet but I just have to say something"? Why, I wonder, did this person try to be silent?

Do people remain silent because they've been taught that disagreement is rude, and conflict isn't to be solved but avoided? Are they too modest to speak, or are they afraid of sounding ill-informed? Or is silence the virtue of fools? (Frances Bacon said this.)

If silence is golden, how do we justify its value during the Salem Witch Trials when the unsuspicious knew better, or during the McCarthy era when political ambition trumped truth and lives were ruined, or during the Holocaust when unspeakable acts were committed on fellow human beings? Silence, it seems, meant assent, and often seems golden, even today.

Personally, I think that we should all "go to where the silence is and say something" (A. Goodman). Two popular mantras, "transparency" and "relationships," are in trouble if they're practiced without candid dialogue. Silence is the antithesis to either a relationship or to transparency because both require trust. Marriage has taught most of us that trust isn't developed in silence.

Relationships shouldn't be confused with networks: one is built on otherness and sharing, and the other on self-interest. Transparency isn't simply putting your best foot forward, but taking the risk of putting it in your mouth.

However, since I've been wrong a couple of times in 80-some years, I began researching what others have said, and I found some evidence that silence is golden in some situations.

For example, silence seems necessary when your son is arguing with his wife, or you'll never see your son again. Sons forgive your point of view; daughters-in-law don't if they think you're aligned with your son. When someone is giving an opinion about religion or their favorite wall hangings, silence is a virtue because both religion and art are very personal and based on emotion more than intellect.

If there's no chance the other person is listening to you or anyone else, such as in political beliefs, silence is the golden pill that prevents heart attacks. Silence is wise when someone wants to tell you more than you want to know since even a nod encourages the long-winded.

It's best to be silent when tempted to give a teenager advice or stories about the old days or when a grown child tells you how to make meatloaf or why you should take it easy, as though that's a measure of enjoyment with only a short time to let out all the stops. Speech is totally unnecessary when you know perfectly well what someone's body language is telling you, and you don't want the person to know that you know.

R.L. Stevenson said the cruelest lies are often told in silence, so you don't want to answer lies about you lest your speech sound defensive or vulnerable.

Finally, silence is golden if you already know the story, especially the punch line, and are passionate about telling it.

Having thought it over, we could concede that though silence isn't golden, neither is speech under certain circumstances.

The research shows that silence is the virtue of fools, but that silence suggests one is a fool while speech confirms it.

We examined dozens of wise sayings and concluded that silence isn't always golden, but neither is speech. So now all we need to do is develop the wisdom to know when silence is golden and when it isn't. Perhaps there's a Golden Book on wisdom called Proverbs.

Hearts or Humours

Centuries ago, humans were thought to be governed by four humours: phlegm, blood, choler (yellow bile) and melancholy (black bile). If the temper of the body was balanced, good humour was achieved; if any one of the humours predominated, the person would be in poor humour, so to speak.

We rarely explain human behavior today by citing the "humours," but we're still inclined to divide our actions according to mind and heart. The good we do supposedly comes from the heart, but that leaves the mind in charge of all the awful things. Actually, if the heart holds the emotions, it seems to be in charge of anything that doesn't make sense, good or bad.

Since what we read in the mass media seems to fall in the category of either maudlin sentiment or mindless violence, I began to wonder what governs or possesses the human species. What, I said to myself, does the heart have to do with it? The heart, individually, is an organ that pumps blood, but when it's used among a group of words, it becomes our dispositions.

The heart is a favored reference among organs. How often is life explained through references to the liver, pancreas, appendix, lungs or tonsils? These words have one meaning, alone or within a group of words, but not the heart. You'd think that every action, except those we're ashamed of, comes from the heart. We can forgive just about anything if we consider it came from the heart.

When we say "you're someone after my own heart," we don't mean your heart comes after mine. We mean you're in tune with us psychologically, mentally, morally. If you reject me, you break my heart, but obviously it mends right away or it wasn't really damaged at all. Otherwise, I'd have a bleeding heart, except that doesn't have anything to do with an injury, but probably indicates that I'm sympathetic and probably a Democrat.

We even give credit to the heart for things that ought to be the province of the brain. We "learn things by heart," which means you probably won't forget it. That pesky brain forgets things, so it's best to learn things by heart. I can still recite "Up and down the beach we flit, one little sandpiper and I, and fast we gather bit by bit, the scattered drift wood, beached and dried." It has no relevance to my life in Wyoming, but has come in handy as an exercise in articulation, which seems to be a lost art nowadays, or an indication that we're deaf. The point is, my mind forgot who wrote it, but my heart remembers it.

The heart even takes on a moral dimension when we cross our hearts to indicate that we're telling the truth. After all, we don't cross our lungs, though we may cross our fingers if we're lying. And if we change our minds, we don't uncross our hearts. We have a change of heart, which means that we just switch to someone else's heart, either through a change in our minds or heart surgery.

One of the disgusting references to the heart is the idea that if we covet something or someone, we "eat our hearts out." That could be the same as "losing heart," but though I may be discouraged if my heart is eaten out, the idiom becomes idiotic if we interchange the meanings.

It's hard to say whether we have too much heart and too little brain, or have simply let the heart substitute for the brain. For example, there are 45 food banks in Casper and that makes our hearts sing with joy, or at least hum with self-satisfaction. Helping the hungry warms the "cockles" of our hearts, but it may also invite a system of fraud, duplicate efforts, low nutritional standards, and helps us forget about international hunger. Besides, cockles either resemble a wrinkled shell or a small shallow boat, so warming them seems to be desirable. Maybe, when solving community problems, it would be better to exercise our minds before engaging our hands, than to wear our hearts on our sleeves before rolling them up.

Personally, I think the only proper use of the heart is to keep a song in it, or is that a song in my soul? I'd rather activate my melancholy than give the cockles of my heart any attention. It's just that all this attention on the heart seems to lead to well-intentioned focus on children, animals and history that trivializes and sentimentalizes the truth. There are days that world events and local police reports activate our black bile, and should. The humours make more sense than warmed cockles, if you think about it. We have little reason to have mindless feelings of pleasure and contentment. I've been on Lake Superior in a shallow boat and I say "out with the cockles!"

Way Back to School

There's no doubt about it: back to school is a marker, a definite transition. But why is it called back instead of forward or onward? Back to school sounds like a big interruption and a loss of momentum in what we're presently doing, and if we think about it, it's just the contrary. By the end of August we're all stalled and looking forward to a new phase, a new season, a new objective.

Personally, I went forward to school for 70 years and I still feel the most comfortable on a campus somewhere. My earliest memories of school are a bit fuzzy, but the feelings aren't hard to resurrect. At five years old, I loved my school because they had books and I had to walk about a mile over country roads and fields to get to them. I had an older brother and sister who usually guided me, though they tended to abandon me on the way home if I was carrying a heavy encyclopedia that weighed me down a bit. At an early age, I evidently thought that the bigger the book, the better the book, and I still browse dictionaries, thesauruses and other references. The descriptions are good and one is free to make up plots. I still like the feel and smell of a book. I concede that Kindles are lighter for trips, but they just don't appeal to my senses the way paper, glue and bindings do.

Most of all, I remember that the country school was by a creek and that chickens ran around in the yard and were available for plucking to make head bands. This was the creek that Sonny pushed me in every day until my father told me to hit him with my lunch box, so I did. Since my father approved, I continued the habit of defending myself into adulthood.

We moved to a small town when I was in 5th grade, to a huge brick school with four rooms and a gymnasium. There was little emphasis on the clothes children wore, since it was the Depression, but the school did have concerns about lice and dirty, smelly kids. My mother reviewed the seating arrangements every year so that dirty George sat at least four seats behind me. She had some influence because she voluntarily used government commodities to make hot lunch casseroles for the children after I complained that we had to drink canned grapefruit juice for nutrition during recess.

The process of returning to school in the fall didn't change too much when I sent my four children off every year. Everyone got new shoes and one new outfit for school. With three boys, clothes were handed down. The one daughter received used clothing from out-of-state friends.

I do recall that tennis shoes for the boys were between $6 and $8 and now the "cheap" ones are between $60 and $80. But clothes weren't a problem as they appear to be now. The "problem" was a daughter who thought that she should wear cowboy boots with a tutu, but I decided that her classmates would take care of that. They didn't, and her next statement of individuality was to create weird hairdos. The most excitement displayed at our house when they were elementary students was the anticipation of seeing all the friends who didn't live on their block, and getting new crayons. Crayons seemed to have a sensory affect on them — the smell, the color, the taste. I was excited for them even though I knew I would have to take a turn on "stinky tennis shoes and bologna" lunch duty in the gymnasium.

We lived on Country Club Road when the children were young, and we insisted that they walk to school. Fairdale Elementary School was three or so blocks over the uninhabited hill. To this day my sons and daughter accuse me of sending them off in snowstorms. I admit that I did, but what they didn't know was that I followed behind to see that they made it. It was one of my character-building exercises … for me, as it turned out. My adult offspring say that as a result of their terror of walking over the Fairdale hill in a storm, they sit by the fireplace during every snowfall, but I think they do because their children are driving in it and they need to stay near the phone, or because they're tired or older than I was at their age.

So it's back to school, and that invites a range of emotions from excitement and delight to fear and loathing, I suppose. It was always something I anticipated after a lazy summer of swimming, having tea parties under the shade tree, sitting in the garden eating raw carrots, playing kick the can and jumping out of the hay mow. By August, I was in another world because there was little I hadn't already done, including reading all day long. The plots from the Hardy Boys and Nancy Drew mysteries and the Alcott books were beginning to run together. I never could read one book at a time.

I miss going back to school, and next year I may do it rather than reminisce about it.

Public Broadcasting: Our Better Selves

Usually, I appreciate George Will's thoughtful columns, even when I don't agree with them. But I was disappointed at his logic in decrying the need for public broadcasting. It just seemed to be out of character; neither his conclusion nor his rationale met his usual standards of clarity and persuasion.

Will contends that public broadcasting is superfluous because public interests don't correspond to people's desires. I shudder to think about where we would be had the Founding Fathers decided that public education should be free in order to fulfill desires. Clearly, they thought that public schools were necessary, free and available to all if our interest in self-government was to be sustained.

One could also say that about public broadcasting. Often public television tells me something I didn't know that either enriches my understanding or enhances my appreciation. Ken Burns' documentaries aren't the result of what people desire, but what people need to know in order to appreciate our heritage and help guide us in making today's decisions.

Will also claims that public television isn't needed because people have thousands of radio and television choices. "There's no scarcity of entertainment" and, therefore, public television is superfluous, he said. He added that Big Bird is designed to please the affluent and their children.

I have a long-time personal interest in public broadcasting. I was involved in the study commission appointed by Governor Ed Herschler in 1978 to find out whether Wyoming needed or wanted public broadcasting. At that time, Wyoming was one of only two states that didn't have a public system.

The first action of the commission was to contract with Dr. John Crawford to conduct a survey of Wyoming citizens on the recommendation of the Wyoming Humanities Council. The idea was to determine the interests and needs of the public so that the legislature could make a decision.

Emphasis was placed not only upon the use of public broadcasting in the schools, but in rural areas. Person-to-person interviews were conducted in Medicine Bow, Burns, Lusk, Manville, Glendo, Glenrock, Midwest, Edgerton, Sundance, Afton, Burlington, Hyattville, Manderson/Pavillion, Shoshoni, Ten Sleep and in every single county. An assumption was made that city folks had access through Colorado and surrounding states, but that rural areas weren't connected.

Over 200 interviews were held, and the majority of those interviewed felt strongly that public broadcasting could provide useful information as well as entertainment that not only informed but was thought-provoking.

As expected, educators in public schools and higher education, members of the Humanities and Art Councils, civic groups and parents felt strongly about the potential use of public broadcasting. What was surprising to the surveyors were the uses that ranchers and farmers thought a public system could serve, not only with information about their challenges, but as a source of communication with other ranchers and farmers.

More than half the people polled agreed that a non-commercial system within the state was important in providing informative programs for children and for adults. Suggestions were made to provide information on many subjects including U.S. history, other cultures, the environment and public policy as well as handicrafts, solar energy, commodity and livestock marketing, range management and the development of natural resources.

The major concern in 1978 was the cost of and whether government would control the content. On the other hand, the major concern with commercial television was the poor quality and the advertising interruptions. There was general agreement about the potential quality and variety of informative programs without commercial sponsorship/ censorship, which are intrinsic to commercial broadcasting.

Most of the respondents in the 1978 survey felt that public television would include cultural events and dramatic ventures as well as educational children's programs and information for a variety of recreational and vocational interests.

The legislature, which had turned down two proposals in the 1960s, approved public broadcasting after studying the survey and upon the recommendation of the commission and several civic groups.

Anyone who has tried to find mature, intelligent and informative programming on commercial television can draw the conclusion that commercial television and radio owners and producers believe that they're meeting the "desires" of the American people. Many of us believe that desires are superficial and that if we scrape away the thin skin of "want" we shall get to the fundamental better nature/needs of all human beings.

Those needs aren't met by commercial broadcasting, but by non-commercial public broadcasting which responds to our better selves. We saw the need for public broadcasting 40 years ago, and we need it even more today than we did then.

Public broadcasting is in the same category as our need for public humanities, art, music and education programs. Citizenship in a representative democracy can't be based on self-interested desires, but upon communal needs and responsibilities.

Common Standards, Common Values

In 2009, governors and state superintendents began working with representative educators, content specialists, researchers, community groups and national organizations from 48 states to develop shared national standards. The idea was to ensure that students in every state are held to the same level of expectations as students in other countries that are educational high performers.

Simply said, common core standards describe what students are expected to know and do at each level of learning. They're common, not because all students are the same, but because every child, every school, every district, every state are in accord not only about what students should know, but what they should be able to do in this century and in this country.

There are those who are objecting to the standards. Some feel that they consist of a common curriculum or instruction; others says that common standards are a communist plot to brainwash children. Others believes that common standards indicate that one-size-fits-all; they use the term "cookie cutter" to indicate a lack of individuality in students and therefore, in instruction; or they believe that it's a "federal" directive and they object to anything "federal."

Ironically, common standards were proposed by state officials, and having common standards requires the recognition of differences in intelligence, in styles of learning and in the time it takes to progress from one stage to another. This, in turn, requires that depth of study is better than trying to cover everything in a limited time space, locked into steps in study rather than steps in learning. Adopting common core standards may have to change our thinking about groupings by age and grade instead of by individual progress. That's the opposite of one-size-fits-all thinking.

The standards have been adopted by Wyoming, and the local district is preparing teachers and schools so that it will now be possible for students to transfer from one school to another without being either bored or lost, or to move from elementary to middle school prepared for the next stage of development ... unless everybody changes their minds, not on the basis of what's appropriate for children, but on the basis of political dogma.

Perhaps spelling out common expectations should have been called "going back to the good ol' days" since core standards once were district-wide. Standards were the core, or central part, of what students learned to be successful intellectually, socially and economically in the world at the time.

What common core standards aren't: they don't dictate a common curriculum if critics mean the same texts and the same lessons, nor do they dictate a common instructional method for every teacher. On the contrary, they challenge each teacher to assess the performance and growth of each child and to redirect each student's efforts in order to move them to the next level.

Why support common standards? Perhaps the simplest answer is so that 18 percent of students have moved during the previous year and school mobility over a three-year period is over 30 percent nationally. With common standards, students can move from one school or state to another and begin where they left off.

Because the standards are based on what students need to know in this century, recognizing individual differences, capabilities and speeds, it means that students explore the subject until they've achieved the skills and knowledge they need in order to go on to the next level. This requires student engagement in the way they learn best.

The career center being planned can be the next step for the Natrona County school district to engage students more thoroughly and encourage them to perform at the level they need in order to achieve success. Not only will the subject matter be connected with the practical application, but the student's pace, learning style, and situation can be assessed as he/she moves toward the standard. Assessments will be used to determine what corrective actions need to be taken to help the student, not for some measure that fortifies adult egos.

When one considers some of the national trends such as a growing senior population and the need for well-educated young men and women, it's imperative to be aware of what our students need to know and be able to do, and then hold them until they succeed in a shrinking, demanding world.

The common standards do have serious implications. Districts will need to be sure that the teachers understand the standards and adjust their instructional expectations and methods to help each child achieve them to the fullest level they can. Core standards will call for teacher preparation, time and space scheduling, student groupings, the connection between knowledge and skills, and the decision-making processes used to respond to rapid change.

When the Natrona County drop-out rate exceeds 25 percent and the university is providing remedial courses to a large proportion of high school graduates, it's obvious that changes needed to be made, even though the top 15 percent in the U.S. compare favorably with every other country in the world and the disadvantaged American students do better than students in other countries. In this country, we take pride in educating ALL students.

Common standards are fundamentally the reflection of our common values. Wyoming students can meet the high standards of students in any other state, and should.

Getting This Straight

Editor's note: A past and present member of the Casper City Council announced their intention to launch a petition campaign to change the local form of government from a council-manager system that has worked for 50 years, to an elected-administrative mayor form of government.

I try to keep up with local, state and national politics, painful as it is. Like most people, I find that local politics seem to make more sense than state and national, but this week the local politicians who propose getting rid of the council-manager form of government aren't making much sense.

It's true that as a member of the League of Women Voters, I was involved in studying and recommending the manager form of government, a nd it also may be true that because it was more than 50 years ago, I could be, as they say of seniors, "losing it."

But when former Councilperson Keith Goodenough and present Councilperson Amanda Huckabay launched an effort to get rid of a system rather than investigate why there has been "turmoil," the reasoning perplexes me.

Did I get it straight? These seem to be the reasons to dump a system that has worked well for more than 50 years:

1) The present "turmoil" is caused by the system;
2) Voters would have more influence if one elected official, rather than seven, was in charge of making decisions;
3) Instead of a group holding one person, the manager, accountable, one person would hold hundreds of employees accountable;
4) The voters would select a mayor with management skills, education and experience;
5) The voters would fire an incompetent mayor since the council couldn't.

But what if the present system encourages council members to study and understand their important roles as setting directions, hiring a skilled manger, holding the manager accountable for results and reflecting the culture and values of the council and community, and making decisions as a group about budgets, goals, regulations, traffic, garbage, etc.?

If the present council, together, can't manage one employee, how will one mayor selected on the basis of his or her competency in getting elected, manage a large and complex enterprise?

What happens when the mayor doesn't manage either the agency or the "turmoil"? Does he serve until his term is over because, unlike a city manager, he can't be terminated without cause by the council? What if voters don't know that the mayor isn't performing very well? Will they elect him for another term just to avoid controversy, i.e. "turmoil"?

What are the advantages of substituting the knowledge, skills and values of one person (mayor) for the collective wisdom of seven people? Have we lost our faith in a representative democracy? Voters do have a direct say about who serves on the council and if they've chosen well, the council in turn will hire the competency needed to run city services on a day-to-day basis.

When the League of Women Voters, who were respected by local, state and national officials, studied and promoted the council-manager form of government, it didn't do so to eradicate turmoil, nor did the voters adopt it for that reason. Casper voters decided that they were growing and needed a professionally-trained person to carry out the visions and goals of the citizens. Casperites elected council members who were respectful, but not deferential; they were assertive, but weren't inclined to think they should interfere with personnel problems. It's true that most of us would agree that the council, in hiring professionals like Erickson and Forslund, didn't hire manipulative, unqualified individuals. Both went on to big state jobs requiring management skills, and both did an excellent job for Casper. Neither, however, hesitated to give informed advice to the council, nor did they ignore ethics in doing so.

Yes, the council members must understand their roles; they must hire carefully and hold people accountable regularly; they must have the will to correct their mistakes if they aren't pleased with manager performance or character.

Most of all, if they can't manage to work together and solve issues collectively, no system change is going to eradicate turmoil. Turmoil, i.e., uncertainty and confusion, is caused by people who have either misunderstood or violated a system.

Before changing the system or signing a petition to radically change how Casper has been administered successfully for many years, both potential petition signers and council members should review how the present system is supposed to work, and then insist that elected officials take responsibility for how the manager fulfills his role.

About the author...

Audrey Cotherman writes periodic columns for the Casper Star-Tribune and Casper Journal, and was publisher and editor of the Dubois Frontier newspaper, which received several awards for editorial excellence. Involved in Wyoming politics and non-profit agencies in Casper, Cheyenne and Laramie since 1961, she served as executive director of the Wyoming Humanities Council and United Way of Natrona County, and was Wyoming Deputy State Superintendent of Public Instruction for 12 years. Cotherman also served on the Natrona County School District Board of Trustees for five years. She resides in Casper, has three sons and a daughter, six grandchildren and two great-grandchildren.

www.ingramcontent.com/pod-product-compliance
Lightning Source LLC
Chambersburg PA
CBHW071919290426
44110CB00013B/1415